T

Two thousand years ago the revered Talmudist Hillel the Elder summed up humanity's most important instruction: "What is hateful to you, do not to your fellow man: all the rest is commentary." Dr Richard Bayer has made an important contribution to that commentary in this book. Dr. Bayer, a theologian, economist, and ethicist, gives us his instruction with respect to "how to live" and how the living of an ethical and good life can become a vital part of restoring a commitment to virtue. Drawing on the religious teachings of various faiths, Dr. Bayer makes a compelling argument for the importance of ethical considerations in business as well as life. As the title suggests, the book is an excellent guidebook for improving one's work and life and goes a long way toward defining what a "good person" is.

SOL WACHTLER,

former Chief Judge of the New York State Supreme Court and Chief Judge of the New York State Court of Appeals.

Judge Wachtler has been awarded thirteen honorary Doctor of Law Degrees, has a chair in Legal Aid named for him at Bar han University in Israel, and chaired the "Law and the Holocaust" Conference in Berlin, Germany.

This book puts a compass and a steering wheel in the hands of anyone who is open to the Spirit and also in need of a fresh start on his or her professional life.

REV. WILLIAM BYRON, S.J.,

an economist & ethicist, past president of the Catholic University of America and author of *A Book of Quiet Prayer.*

Rev. Byron is the former director of The Center for the Advanced Study of Ethics and distinguished professor of management at Georgetown University.

Richard Bayer brings the learning of a theologian to bear on the everyday experience of workers striving to succeed in today's economy. Readers will find here tools that contribute to economic success, to be sure. But they will also find wisdom that leads to the understanding and attainment of a fuller and more satisfying kind of success. Bayer clarifies the choices before us and challenges us to take the route to true human fulfillment. He writes as one who is well on the way.

KEVIN SCHMIESING,
Book Review Editor, *Journal of Markets & Morality*

Good ethical thinking always returns to basic principles. Plato's key question was, "How ought I live?" Should I seek the pleasurable, the useful, or the good? Another tradition tells us that the good by its nature is to be done, and the evil avoided. Throughout his book, Richard Bayer calls us back to basic principles. In chapter after chapter, he confronts a problem in business with a fundamental principle of ethics, and he shows how right ethical principles should—indeed, must—be applied. His chapters on the virtues will intrigue any reader. Can a company seminar discuss prudence, justice, courage, temperance? Is there place for human dignity, kindness, wisdom? Most of all, Richard Bayer's book is not a set of answers, but a set of challenges: again and again, the reader will say, "I'll have to think about that." And there's the value of this book.

JOSEPH T. LIENHARD, S.J.,
Professor, Fordham University

Richard Bayer has produced an insightful and thought provoking primer on the subject of personal and business ethics. It is objective and practical with regard to the theory of ethical behavior but deals with this complex subject in an easy to read and understandable way. It reminds the reader of the strong, ethical underpinnings this country was founded on as opposed to today, when personal and business mores appear to be in significant decline. The text also speaks clearly to the practical necessity of keeping our ethical values in place if we are to continue to be a nation of freedom, equality, and human dignity. Anyone engaged in the study of ethics and individuals, educational institutions or businesses desiring to do so, would be well advised to consider this text because of its sound theory, practicality, and readability.

BILL LEE,
former EVP and CFO, Interfirst Bank, Houston, Texas

A must read and a great reference as we navigate our personal and professional lives.

JIM WEIHROUCH,
author of *Joy at Work*

The Good Person Guidebook

Transforming Your
Personal Life

The Good Person Guidebook

Transforming Your Personal Life

RICHARD BAYER, Ph.D.

With a Foreword by Kate Wendleton

Five O'Clock Club Books
www.FiveOClockClub.com

The Good Person Guidebook: Transforming Your Personal Life by Richard Bayer, Ph.D.

Copyright ©2008 The Five O'Clock Club,® Inc.
Some of the contents of this work appeared previously in somewhat different form in other
Five O'Clock Club® works. The Five O'Clock Club®, Seven Stories Exercise and Forty-Year
Vision are registered trademarks of The Five O'Clock Club®, Inc.
Printed in Canada

1 2 3 4 5   09 08 07 06
Five O'Clock Books is a part of The Five O'Clock Club, Inc.
For more information contact Five O'Clock Books,
300 East 40th Street, New York, NY 10016 · 212-286-4500
Or find us on the World Wide Web at www.FiveOClockClub.com

Library of Congress Cataloging-in-Publication Data
Bayer, Richard
The Good Person Guidebook: Transforming Your Personal Life /by Richard Bayer, Ph.D., with
foreword by Kate Wendleton
p. m.
Includes index.
    Contents: Pt. 1. A perspective on ethics—pt. 2. Virtue: what type of person should we
be?—

pt. 3. Guidelines: what must we do (ethical principles for action).
    ISBN 978-0-944054-16-1

    1. Conduct of life. 2. Ethics. 3. Virtue. I. Title.

BJ1581.2.B365 2008
170'.44—dc22   2006045614

NOTICE TO THE READER
Publisher does not warrant or guarantee any of the products described herein or perform any
independent analysis in connection with any of the product information contained herein.
Publisher does not assume, and expressly disclaims, any obligation to obtain and include
information other than that provided to it by the manufacturer.

    The reader is expressly warned to consider and adopt all safety precautions that might be
indicated by the activities herein and to avoid all potential hazards. By following the instructions
contained herein, the reader willingly assumes all risks in connection with such instructions.

    The Publisher makes no representation or warranties of any kind, including but not
limited to, the warranties of fitness for particular purpose or merchantability, nor are any such
representations implied with respect to the material set forth herein, and the publisher takes no
responsibility with respect to such material. The publisher shall not be liable for any special,
consequential, or exemplary damages resulting, in whole or part, from the readers' use of, or
reliance upon, this material.

President, The Five O'Clock Club: Kate Wendleton
Chief Operating Officer: Richard C. Bayer, Ph.D.
SVP, Director of the Guild of Career Coaches: David Madison, Ph.D.
Cover Design: Andrew Newman Design
Interior Design and Production: Bookwrights Design

To my wife, Catherine, whose support made this book possible,
and
to Sara, Paul, and Mart,
whom we hope we are helping to form into good persons.

Our culture is at a critical cusp—a time that requires that we define what it means to be a citizen in a democracy. Within our nation we need to foster a greater sense of collective responsibility.

Robert Bellah, author

Foreword

He was, after all, a good father
—that is to say, an ineffective man.
Real goodness was different, it was irresistible, murderous,
it had victims like any other aggression;
in short, it conquered.

James Salter, *Light Years*

A person is often described as "good" when he's simply agreeable: "He's a good Joe"; "a good fellow." But that's not *real* goodness. Good combats evil. Evil is strong, aggressive, unflinching. Goodness must be even stronger and more aggressive to fight evil, or what use is it? Real goodness is determined, driven, resourceful, focused. Real goodness is relentless. It has strength, sets standards, influences others. Real goodness is a force, however quiet it may be.

A genuinely good person is a person of moral excellence, but not in a vacuum. A good person is good for the community. In an obituary, a newspaper described a certain wealthy man as a good person. He did well for himself, made a nice living, and often took his daughter sailing on his boat. But whom had he cared for outside of his immediate family? No one. What they described was not a *good* person, but a selfish one.

Companies can also be good in a similar sense as people are good: caring for their employees and taking care of their communities. The Five O'Clock Club tries to be a good corporate citizen. For ten years, we ran a program for disadvantaged adults in Harlem, helping them get into careers and not just jobs.

At present, the Club brings educational programs to a local prison, and Richard Bayer was one of the first in that program. Although he taught economics and ethics at the college level for twenty years, he now teaches college math and GED math to inmates because that's what they need. In fact, officials at the prison said they had never *seen* inmates so excited about math as they did when Richard taught them. He is not only competent; but he also teaches with commitment and love, and the students respond to it. He is a *good* teacher in the real sense of the word.

He has empathy. He says that the people there have already been taken down a notch. His job is not just to teach them math, but also to encourage them, raise their spirits, and give them hope. When I started my own prison teaching,

instructing inmates on how to have their own small businesses (as a representative of The Five O'Clock Club), Richard
gave me some ideas so I would be sure to treat the attendees
with the dignity and respect they deserve. As you will see in
this book, treating people with dignity means that we see
and treat them as fragile, social, free and creative, and equal,
among other things. No wonder Richard had 100% attendance every week. He even got permission to hold a small
party the last day of class!

In addition to providing teachers, The Club contributes
financially to the prison education program, and we've developed a small-business library in the prison. Doing this work
gives us energy for the other parts of our lives. Yes, virtue is
its own reward, as you will see in the chapters to come.

Finally, The Five O'Clock Club is guided by traditional
religious ethics, and we say so. This statement can be shock-
ing at first to prospective corporate clients. But we do not
mean by this that we espouse or support any particular religion, church, or sectarian movement; *nor is religion ever mentioned at our meetings*—which are attended by Christians,
Jews, Muslims, and people of other faiths. But we *are* guided
by *traditional religious ethics,* which translates simply into
*always doing what is in the best interest of job hunters and
employees.*

This approach resonates with other good corporate citizens,
hence we count as our clients such companies as Scholastic,
Time-Warner, major law firms, hospitals, not-for-profits,

prestigious financial services companies, and large and small manufacturing companies, among others. Our emphasis on ethics means that our focus is not just our own bottom line. It means that we pass up possible publicity if the story may hurt employees (negative stories are the norm). It also means that we will continue to work with employees even after they have gotten a new job—just to make sure they do well in that job.

The public is hungry for information about how to be a good person. The Five O'Clock Club publishes a monthly magazine, *The Five O'Clock News,* focusing on career-related topics. In fact, our approach to job hunting is methodical, pragmatic, and meant to help people get the best jobs quickly and do well in their present jobs. However, Richard's occasional column in our magazine, *Practical Religion,* has been the most popular series with our readers. We have found that our readers don't want just job-hunt and career-development tips; they also want to know how to live. For example, in Richard's articles, they learn from Buddhism how to overcome suffering. Islam teaches them how to stay focused. And Christianity gives them a surprising definition of love ("Love means to intend the good of the other."). You will find these articles and more in this book.

Richard is a theologian, an economist, and an ethicist. He is also a great businessman and serves as the Chief Operating Officer of The Five O'Clock Club. He helps our business stay healthy so we can help others. We are proud to include his book in our series.

I am not sure exactly what heaven will be like,
but I know that when we die and it comes time
for God to judge us,
He will NOT ask, How many good things have you
done in your life?, rather he will ask,
How much LOVE did you put into what you did?

Mother Teresa

And, as we know from Richard, "love" means to "intend the good of the other." Study this book and you will be as inspired by Richard as I am every day.

Kate Wendleton
President, The Five O'Clock Club
A national career coaching and outplacement organization
www.FiveOClockClub.com

Preface

There are only two great questions that arise in ethical theory:

- "What type of person should I *be?*" and
- "What should I *do* given a decision of ethical importance?"

To answer these questions, a person requires some sort of ethical perspective. For example, you could take your ethical perspective from the movie "Wall Street" where Gordon Gekko passionately tells us why "greed is good."

In this book, however, I use both philosophical and traditional religious ethics to help us to answer these questions. Your personal ethics will affect both your work and your personal life.

In the *Good Person Guidebook*, you will learn the compatibility of good ethics and success. You will discover the character traits that help you to get along at work and in your personal life and help to make you happy. You will get answers to the questions, "Who should I be?" and "What must I do?"

This book is divided into three parts:
- · an overall perspective on ethics (Part I),
- · ethics pertaining to one's character (Part II), and
- · putting ethical principles into action (Part III).

Everyone needs ethics. People generally have little problem seeing that ethics pertains to our personal life. However, some consider "economic ethics" to be an oxymoron. I strongly disagree! Those of us with full-time jobs spend a large part, if not *most*, of our waking hours at work. So we cannot leave our ethics at the doorstep when we put on our hats as employees if we consider ourselves to be people of good ethics!

Some people may be driven by "greed is good," but in this book I assume that the classical virtues of justice, prudence, courage, and temperance are still applicable today. Beyond those virtues we also examine hope, humility, thrift, compassion, and other lesser virtues. Indeed, their applications are both useful and even delightful in guiding us as we answer the character question, "What type of person should I be?" In expounding on the topics pertaining to work and personal life I use religious and philosophical thought. As for religious thought, the reader will not find this book to be a "sectarian" work, but one that relies on some of the best that each tradition has to offer. Consequently, I rely on Christianity,

Judaism, Buddhism, and Islam to help to answer the two main questions in ethics.

Unfortunately, I can give you no *comprehensive* answer as to what a good person is and would do in all settings. Methodological honesty and humility prohibit any such monumental comprehensive claim. That answer would depend on your station in life: business, family, friends, and obligations. However, I do indeed offer important advice on various situations that occur in most people's lives:

· How can you overcome suffering?
· How does ethics fit into your work life?
· What is the real meaning of love? How do you show that you love someone?
· Where does compassion fit in our lives?
· What is the value of thrift as a virtue?
· How important is freedom and what does it mean to be "free"?
· When should you blow the whistle on your employer?!

These are just some of the topics covered. The chapters are interesting in themselves and thought provoking for the reader.

A Study Guide

In fact, some groups use this text as a basis for discussion. The chapters run from 2 to10 pages each and need not be taken in sequence. A study group can select the topics of most interest to them and discuss one per week. To understand the material thoroughly, it is helpful to discuss it.

The *Good Person Guidebook* tackles many questions concerning personal and business behavior, and is a terrific text for adult study groups in religious- and ethics-oriented organizations.

This is an easy entry for organizations that want to work with adults. You can help your members be happier in their personal lives, understand the importance of having a generous spirit and being grateful for what they have. They can also bring spirituality into their jobs, be happier in their work, do right by their fellow employees, and know when to blow the whistle!

The discussions will help readers appreciate the need for good ethics, and discover different ways to approach ethical decision-making. Remember that it is the nature of ethics that there is rarely "one way or answer" to highly complex issues, and so members of a discussion group can enlighten one another. It is in this spirit that I offer the questions that follow each chapter.

Richard Bayer, Ph.D.
New York, 2008

Contents

Part Two: Virtue: What Type of Person Should I Be?

Part Three: Guidelines: What Must We Do (Ethical Principles for Action)

Part 1

A Perspective
on Ethics

*To you is granted the power of degrading
yourself into the lower forms of life, the beasts,
and to you is granted the power, contained in
your intellect and judgment, to be reborn into
the higher forms, the divine.*

Giovanni Pico della Mirandola 1463–1494,
Italian Renaissance philosopher,
scholar, and humanist

Introduction

Cheshire Puss, asked Alice. Would you tell me, please, which way I ought to go from here? That depends a good deal on where you want to go, said the Cat. I don't much care where, said Alice. Then it doesn't matter which way you go, said the Cat.

Lewis Carroll, *Alice's Adventures in Wonderland*

thical questions simply cannot be approached without some *perspective or framework* to answer the questions that arise. So the first part of this book equips the reader with perspectives on ethics with which to answer the two major questions in ethics ("What sort of person should I be?", and "What must I do?"). This part addresses topics such as how to overcome suffering, and the traits of humility, compassion and others, as well as issues such as how to make ethical decisions in business. The concept of human dignity serves as an organizing principle.

As mentioned in the preface, the book is divided into three parts:

1. An overall perspective on ethics;

2. Ethics pertaining to one's character ("What sort of person should I be?"); and

3. Ethical principles pertaining to action ("What must I do?").

I hope the reader will enjoy reading about ethical perspective and will find some structural assistance in approaching ethical issues.

✐✐✐ Group Discussion Questions

• Can you name the two basic questions in ethics by memory?

• Do you think that the many ethical questions that we all face are covered by what I call the two basic questions in ethics? ✐✐✐

1

Ethics in the Information Age: The Puritan Work Ethic and Beyond

Flourishing is the meaning and the purpose of life, the whole aim and end of human existence.

Aristotle

hilosophers and other great thinkers have always believed that there are just two major questions in ethics: "What am I to do?," and "Who am I to be?" I want to talk about the latter question here, since it is the more basic one, and it really is about our character. Certain character traits are overwhelmingly important for success in our personal lives, and in business. One gets a sense of that from reading David Madison's section in Part II of this book, *Five O'Clock Clubbers Talk about Their Good Habits*.

We're all familiar with the Puritan work ethic, which was historically, the ethical underpinning for American life, both in the home and at work. The Puritan ethic answered the question, "Who am I to be?" with: "I am to be honest, hard working, reliable, sober, mindful of the future, appropriate in my relationships, successful, and thereby give glory to God."

Today, these character traits are usually thought about, but are only paid lip service. This is because their roots in giving glory to God are no longer as widely accepted (to put it mildly). Since many Americans have given God a back seat, this makes it hard to instill these ideals in others, especially in the young. Without a belief in glorifying God, it's difficult to give others a reason why they should be ethical. Virtues today are like dying plants that have had their roots cut. Virtues are no longer nourished, and are even being deeply challenged, especially in our materialistic and selfish society. The Puritan virtues are dying on the vine almost everywhere—except in some small communities.

People who base their ethics on theological ideas should, of course, keep doing so. This is not to say that we should return to days when there was a greater unity in the belief about God and in business ethics. There are, however, issues of "overlapping consensus"—that is, matters in which almost all of us can agree upon what is ethical.

What this all boils down to is human dignity. Dignity in one's personal life and dignity in the workplace. Protecting and supporting human dignity is the guiding principle behind ethics for many writers, institutions (including the United

Nations), philosophers, religious leaders (such as the Dalai Lama and the Pope), and theologians. So, in the twenty-first century, we can answer the question, "Who am I to be?" The answer is, "I am to be respectful of human dignity in all of its material, emotional, and spiritual aspects."

In the workplace, this means being cooperative, responsible, socially conscious, hard working, fair minded, and honest, so we can protect and promote human dignity. Acting this way at work doesn't solve all of our ethical work-related problems, but it's a start, and a good way to think about difficult issues. For example, when an employee is about to be terminated, the employer should be clear about what is necessary to protect the dignity and future of all parties involved. This includes other workers in the company, as well as the employee's family. The section in Part III entitled, "How to Terminate Employees While Respecting Human Dignity," provides tips and guidelines for acting ethically when someone is let go at work.

Human Dignity in the Information Age

A key to ethical behavior is the virtues to nurture shown in the table below (as well as the vices to avoid). These virtues and vices are consistent with a meaningful work life. Like the Puritan work ethic, these virtues concern themselves with both character ethics and efficiency. They contribute to a thriving and productive work environment.

Table of Virtues vs. Vices

Virtues: Consistent with the Vision	Vices: Inconsistent with the Vision
Cooperation	Excessive competitiveness
Hard work, persistence	Entitlement mentality; workaholic
Creative and optimistic	Zero-sum mentality
Planning	Indifference and haphazard methods
Regard for the welfare of others	Out-of-context behavior
Trust in the future	Siege mentality
Flexibility	Rigid, unable to cope with change
Activity based on knowledge	Disconnected activity
Sharing, generous, patient for long-term results	Closed and possessive approach. Focused on short-term interests

◢ ◢ ◢ **Question(s) to consider**: It's often difficult to assess ourselves and our progress. Imagine a scale rating ethical behavior from 1 to 10, 10 being the most ethical. Anything above 5 is positive; anything below it is negative. As you go through the day, rate your behavior on this scale. Don't nit pick and rate every little thing, but every so often, ask yourself, How would I rate myself so far? Doing this for a week or so can give you a clearer perspective on how good/ethical you are, and how you are progressing. *◢*

A Matter of Responsibility

It is easy to dodge our responsibilities, but we cannot dodge the consequences of dodging our responsibilities.

Josiah Charles Stamp

Our age has produced two types of generally unhappy people: workaholics and those with an entitlement mentality. An exaggerated sense of responsibility for one's future produces the workaholic; a failure of responsibility produces someone who feels a sense entitlement. Both types can hurt an organization's culture, not to mention those in the person's personal life.

Ideally, we all should take on the appropriate amount of responsibility in regard to our jobs and personal lives. But, remember, taking on responsibility for *everything* in our lives is just too much to handle. Though it may seem strange to say this, its truth is clear when we recognize our inability to control much of what happens to us, and how paralyzing it is constantly to worry about the future (however, for those who are believers, there is solace in being in God's care). So, today, to live a happy life, anyone who is irresponsible or lazy should try to work harder and develop him/herself professionally. The reverse is true for workaholics—which means giving up some of their control. Our goal must be to stay in between these extremes—to stay at the center, to achieve a balance. (See Table below)

Social Virtue

In ancient times, land was the basis for production and economic power. To own land meant being able to meet the need for food and shelter, as well as being in power. Indeed, even today severely uneven distribution of land is still a problem in underdeveloped countries. Because of this, many of the world's poor go without food or shelter.

In more recent times, however, capital became the basis for production and economic power. Those with it have had an advantage over labor, that is, people who have only their own labor to sell. The uneven distribution of capital remains a problem in many modern economies.

These days, we sometimes call the U.S. economy a "postmodern" one. This means that knowledge and access to it are becoming the main bases for productivity and economic power. In a real sense, we have entered a new era.

Two Types of Generally Unhappy People

Type of Person	Attitude Toward the Future	Sense of Responsibility	Most Likely Long-Term Prospects
Workaholic	Fearful	Very high	Burnout
Entitlement mentality	Reckless indifference	Very low	Failure
Well-adjusted person	Confident	Strong	Sustainable progress and success

🖉🖉🖉 **Question(s) to consider**: Quickly list the ten most important things in your life, such as your job, time with your kids, keeping up with business, helping out your spouse, etc. Now, rank them and see how much time and attention you pay to each. Ask yourself: Am I living the kind of life that I want to? Am I happy? Don't spend a lot of time on this—it's just to raise your consciousness a bit. 🖉

Sharing knowledge is sharing productive capacity and power. Such sharing allows others to grow and advance, while those who share it also prosper. This is not only a worthy goal in human relations, but it is also a practical necessity, especially considering what's available on the Internet. Partnerships are formed—frequently without money changing hands—to share information (and access to it) to the advantage of both parties.

🖉🖉🖉 **Question(s) to consider**: Pick a topic or skill at work. Do you give as much to others as you get? For example, someone gives you a tip on how better to make travel arrangements. When a new computer system is installed, do you tell him/her about a shortcut you have found? 🖉

Land, labor, knowledge. Human power and prestige have been, and continue to be, tied to all of these commodities. And, still, there's the continuing need for ethical systems to promote and protect human dignity—no matter what the source of power or environment.

*All human beings are born free and equal in
dignity and rights. They are endowed with reason
and conscience and should act towards one another
in a spirit of brotherhood.*

On December 10, 1948 the General Assembly
of the United Nations adopted and proclaimed
the Universal Declaration of Human Rights

✒✒✒ Group Discussion Questions

• Discuss the Puritan work ethic. Do you agree that its virtues are "dying on the vine?"

• Do you think that centering a new work ethic around "human dignity" makes sense and that enough people would agree to this?

• Critically discuss the "new" virtues and vices for today.

• Of course, there are many types of unhappy and happy people. However, relating to work, do you agree with the "happiness" table in this chapter? Do you fit into one of the categories? Do you know others who do? ✒✒✒

2

Our Social Nature

*We are concerned that individualism may have grown
cancerous—that it may be destroying those social integuments
moderating its more destructive potentialities, that it may be
threatening the survival of freedom itself.*

Robert N. Bellah et al., *Habits of the Heart*

One popular approach—which is supported by The Five O'Clock Club—puts human dignity at the center of ethics. This method views a human being as having the following characteristics: material, spiritual, social, fragile, free and creative, and equal. You'll see mentions to these characteristics throughout this book. Whatever promotes genuine human development and well being in these aspects is correct ethically, and those things that do not are ethically wrong. In this chapter, we'll look more closely at our social nature. The table below defines the six characteristics of all of us.

Human beings have been called social animals. There is a close connection between our thriving and our social nature.

Therefore, it is an end in itself for us to belong to families, neighborhoods, churches, professional associations, town communities, civic organizations, and other associations that help fulfill our social nature. It's important to us how we can do this today, and how well this works for each of us. We need proper expression of our social needs.

Characteristics of Human Beings	Definition
1. Material	A person requires food, clothing shelter, etc., to survive.
2. Spiritual	A person must have "space" to practice spirituality.
3. Social	A person only develops to his/her fullest with others.
4. Fragile	We are all prone to error, have our weaknesses, and our failings.
5. Free and creative	We all want to move forward professionally, to exercise our creative abilities.
6. Equal	We all have a basic equality, regardless of race, color, creed, etc.

Giving Our Social Nature Proper Expression Today

Of course, the modern world no longer offers us the sense of nearness and closeness offered by the premodern village. Michael Novak, a theologian and sociologist, claims that we need not regret the passing of these little lost communities.

Novak asks us to consider positively the new, but not yet unappreciated forms of community:

I do not think that anyone has grasped clearly enough the spiritual ideal behind the new forms of voluntary association—the new communitarian ideal—involved in liberal societies. The most distinctive invention of the spirit of capitalism is not the individual as much as it is many individuals joining together in creative enterprise. It is, for example, the joint stock company, the corporation; or again, the credit union, as well as insurance funds and pension funds; and finally, the market itself, considered as a social mechanism obliging all who participate in it to practice a sensible regard for others ... In actual practice, such (liberal) societies exhibit the most highly and complexly organized forms of life in all of human history.

(Novak, *The Catholic Ethic*, p. 27)

Novak's point is well taken. Most of us no longer live in small, closely knit villages. This means that we need to appreciate the new forms of community when these forms meet our genuine needs, rather than longing for the small towns of yesterday. While what Novak says does hold a lot of truth, it's a bit too hasty to say that these newer communities can seriously fulfill our social nature.

When we speak about community in the fullest sense, we're not talking about what sociologists call "enclaves," which people form on the basis of their common needs, interests, and/or lifestyles. There are important *differences* between many of these newer communities and community in the fuller sense. These differences are *commitment* and *memory*. This means that we find fulfillment through joining communities not just on the basis of self-interest, but out of commitment to others within the community, plus, we know that joining serves the common good. For example, it's been long known that workers join labor unions not only for self-interest, but also for solidarity with other workers, and to contribute to the common good in their pursuit of justice. Finally, memory lends continuity and identity to social groups.

If we want a close association—a feeling of unity—with one another, then the so-called enclaves ought not to rule social life. What's essential is personal commitment, commitment to one another as persons, and commitment of the community to the wider common good. These types of commitment shine when we come together in our traditional structures—our families, neighborhoods, parishes, professional associations, and other such groups. The family, for example, is, of course, an important social, and ethical unit. Societies cherish the lasting commitment among members of a family. And don't forget the importance (ideally) of the life-long commitment of marriage, "Until death do we part." Also, the mutual commitment within the family is not closed and self-centered, but spreads out, greatly contributing to the life of society overall. The family is an ethical unit in which conjugal love, fidelity, and the training of children in love, hope, courage, faith, and justice are all indispensable to society. Similarly, we expect various civic groups, at the very least, to foster our commitment to one another and to the common good. Finally, it is certainly true that *professional organizations (such as those made up of nurses, lawyers, teachers, and doctors) not only promote the mutual benefit of their members, but also hold the common good as a major consideration in all of their activities and decisions.*

> 🖉🖉🖉 **Question(s) to consider**: Pick a group you belong to—it could even be your marriage, your department at work or an outside organization. Are you as committed as you can be, that is, are you aware of your responsibilities and how well you fulfill them? Is there some little thing you could do to increase your commitment? 🖉

Certainly, organizations such as corporations, credit unions, and insurance and pension funds all contribute to society. However, they fall far short of a personal social ideal, since they do little to promote commitment.

Not only do the new forms of community fall short, but also the traditional communities are withering away. High divorce rates shatter marriages and wreck what might be a safe soil for the development of children. *We hear more and more that even the professions are no longer serving the common good, as they should.* Even our friendships get ripped apart because many of us often move from city to city, either to take a company promotion or because we can just make more money somewhere else. Even membership in Parent-Teacher Associations is at an all time low. We can hold the moral cultural, political, and economic sectors responsible for this erosion. So, we have a twofold problem. On the one hand, the so-called traditional groups (here, we mean the family, as well as the town, the church, and more) are losing this sense of commitment, while, on the other hand, many of the new social organizations have done little to achieve it.

Toward Reform

What can be done to solve this problem? Society must seriously understand our social nature, and incorporate memory and commitment in our social groups; also we must ensure that we act so that people can thrive—thrive in the broadest sense.

> *🖉🖉🖉* **Question(s) to consider**: Are you doing your part to keep a community alive? What community? How? Is it a community where you actually see or talk to people (as opposed to a virtual community)? *🖉🖉🖉*

There is no quick and easy solution that can be set down by social planners, or even by government. Renewing and transforming communities happens by voluntary actions in our society. Therefore, our churches, civic organizations, and families, should all reassert their active commitment to their members and to the common good.

We were born to unite with our fellow men,
and to join in community with the human race.

Cicero

The life I touch for good or ill will touch another life,
and that in turn another, until who knows where the trembling
stops or in what far place my touch will be felt.

Frederick Buechner

✐✐✐ Group Discussion Questions

• This chapter explores the concept of human dignity. Does the list of characteristics seem correct?

• Can you add any items to the list? ✐✐✐

3

Law vs. Ethics:
The Limits of Law

Human law does not prohibit every vice from which virtuous men abstain, but only graver vices from which the majority of men can abstain.

An Aquinas Reader, Image Books,
Edited by Mary T. Clark, p.372, 1972.

*L*aw vs. ethics? Doesn't that sound strange? Don't they always go together? Ethics goes much further than law, and law alone will never be able to protect the common good. Consider a fairly recent example: the Sarbanes-Oxley Act, passed in 2002. In a nutshell, this law is designed to protect investors, and the common good generally, from those who would unscrupulously profit at the expense of others.

    ♪ ♪ ♪ **Question(s) to consider**: Is there something you are unethically "getting away with" even though it is within the law? How does it make you feel? *♪*

But laws alone can't protect the common good. There are always people who somehow get around a law because they fail in regard to ethics:

- People at the top of the organization try to stay one step ahead of a law by figuring out ways around it. This action likely results in more rounds of legislation, on and on, and on.
- We even can't be sure that those below the top of an organization will not undermine their leaders for their own purposes. Think of divisional heads who have a vested interest in massaging the numbers to make their divisions look good. This misreporting is simply passed upward.
- New opportunities will always come about for the dishonest. Remember the dot.com boom of the 1990s and the economic havoc it caused. Many lost millions due to bad or misleading reporting and shoddy business plans.

We must come up with something beyond the patchwork of laws that result from a combination of compromises and the pressures brought by special interests.

While clearly necessary, law alone will never be able fully to protect the common good. So, if investors, executives, managers, professionals, consumers, and the common good generally are to be protected, we must put in place something beyond the patchwork of laws fashioned by a combination of compromise and the pressures brought by special interests. Legislation tends, at best, to be curative (it fixes problems or punishes) and coercive (it forces people to do things, or not do them).

What we need are business people who practice good behavior. That is, those who don't go after personal, ill-gotten gain at the expense of others. Is this ideal unrealistic, empty, and something that we should forget about? Has civilization dismissed this idea throughout history? No—just the opposite; society has only recently dismissed this idea and, to the harm of business.

We need business people who actually practice good behavior.

The truth is that ethical considerations have been around much longer than have free markets, Adam Smith, the Industrial Revolution, the Internet, and most certainly Sarbanes-Oxley! We can look back thousands of years to philosophical and religious traditions that have formed our (and other) cultures to our benefit. The philosophical traditions (in this case, virtue theory) that have impacted culture go at least as far back as Plato (427–327 B.C.) and Aristotle (384–322 B.C.). So have Buddhism, Hinduism, Judaism, Christianity and Islam, which influence culture and, of course, financial dealings. Indeed, when we think of ethics and economics, the famous sociologist Max Weber (1864–1920) comes to mind. In "The Protestant Ethic and the Spirit of Capitalism," Weber pointed out the importance of Protestantism for the rise of the market in Western culture.

Today, many speak of the "protection and promotion of human dignity" as a path to modern ethics. In any case, the point is clear: throughout history people have valued continuous ethical reflection, even, unfortunately, in the negative way. How often have we heard managers say that "ethics and economics" don't go hand in hand. Still, as you approach higher levels of large organizations, at least lip service is paid to the need for ethics.

> **Ethical reflection has been around much longer than free markets, the Industrial Revolution, and the Internet.**

Ethics can point us toward right action in business and in our personal lives. Ethics can infuse an organization in a way that law does not. As generations before us have, we must put more emphasis on real and enduring ethics if we are to protect the common good.

The state is currently spending five times more for the education for a white child than it is fitting to educate a colored child. That means better textbooks for that child than for that child. I say that's a shame, but my opponent says today is not the day for whites and coloreds to go to the same college. To share the same campus. To walk into the same classroom. Well, would you kindly tell me when that day is gonna come? Is it going to come tomorrow? Is it going to come next week? In a hundred years? Never? No, the time for justice, the time for freedom, and the time for equality is always, is always right now!

From the movie, *The Great Debaters*,
starring Denzel Washington. Screenplay by Robert Eisele.
Based on a true story that took place in 1935.

✎✎✎ Group Discussion Questions

- Explain the part of the title to the chapter which says "...The Limits of Law." What does it mean?

- Why do we need good ethics? What has it to do with the common good? ✎✎✎

4

How to Overcome Suffering—Especially in Your Career

From that hour Siddhartha ceased to fight against his destiny.
There shone in his face the serenity of knowledge, of one
who is no longer confronted with conflict of desires, who has
found salvation, who is in harmony with the stream of events,
with the stream of life, full of sympathy and compassion,
surrendering himself to the stream, belonging to
the unity of things.

Hermann Hesse, *Siddhartha*

At The Five O'Clock Club we participate actively in the career aspects of our clients' lives. This puts us in a great position to make suggestions that can help the employed and unemployed. These same lessons apply to a person's personal life.

Our coaches across the country have noted what we call the unhappiness factor. Many people are unhappy in their professional careers for a variety of reasons. Indeed, they often describe themselves as actually suffering in their present positions. These complaints can include:

- I need more money! $250,000 is simply not enough to support my family.
- I am single, 43, work very long hours, and like having things my way. I definitely intend to have children, but have yet to start looking for the right man/woman.
- Everyone else seems to be moving ahead of me. I live very nicely, but feel left behind and I want more.

🖉🖉🖉 **Question(s) to consider:** On a scale of 1 to 10, 10 being the unhappiest, where do you fall? What's the major thing that stands in the way of your being happier? *🖉*

We can learn a lot by analyzing these situations in light of Eastern traditions. Buddhism talks about suffering as much as any religion does.

Many people love the story of the Buddha, which means "Enlightened One." He was born Siddhartha Gautama and lived in northern India from 560 to 480 B.C. Gautama's family was wealthy, yet he himself was unhappy with the pleasures of the royal life. So, as a young fellow, he left his wife and son, and sneaked out of the palace and into the woods to become enlightened about the true meaning of life. Pleasure did not seem to be the key to a happy life.

After practicing yoga under religious masters, he concluded that it is best to avoid extreme asceticism. These masters followed a life of extreme self-denial to the point of begging for food and dressing in rags. Buddha finally left this sect and came to his moderate approach (the "middle way" between extreme asceticism and extravagance) while meditating for 49 days under a bo tree. Once he had achieved such enlightenment, he returned to ordinary life for the sake of others.

He was a compassionate teacher with a cool head and a warm heart. Once enlightened, the Buddha came to understand four things:

First, suffering is a part of life. There are the traumas of birth, sickness, old age, fear of death, separation from loved ones, etc. There is passing, constant change, and mortality.

To be sure that your goals (desires) will bring you happiness and not suffering, analyze them for their wisdom and compassion.

Second, unreasonable desires or expectations cause suffering. Failing to show wisdom, restraint or compassion, people cling to what is either too much or can never be permanent. People can put themselves at the center of the world, and become intoxicated with themselves and their desires. They seek permanence and an ease of life that are impossible to have. They look out for their own welfare without having compassion for others, or regard for the rest of the world.

> *I slept and dreamt that life was joy.*
> *I awoke and saw that life was service.*
> *I acted and behold, service was joy.*

> Rabindranath Tagore, philosopher, author,
> songwriter, painter, educator, composer,
> Nobel laureate (1861-1941)

🖋🖋🖋 **Question(s) to consider**: Do you have any unreasonable desires or expectations that are causing you to suffer? What are they? Are you simply looking out for your own welfare without having compassion for others or regard for the rest of the world? Specifically, how do you look out for others? Are you satisfied with what and how much you are doing? 🖋

Third, the good news is this: Overcoming desire can break the chain of suffering.

Fourth, the way to overcome desire is through a life of wisdom and practical compassion (as taught by the "Eightfold Path").

So, a Buddhist would analyze the three complaints of our suffering employees in terms of the wisdom and compassion that they do or do not show:

~ If you "need" more than $250,000, are you cling-
  ing to what is really unreasonable, unfulfilling, and
  passing? (The median per capita income in this
  country is after all about $32,400!). Does your
  preoccupation show a lack of compassion for the
  99.99% of the planet's population that has less?
  Have you considered the middle way, living in between the extremes of poverty and riches?

~ If you are single and insist on having things your
  way, have you put yourself at the center of the
  world? Are you too used to seeing yourself falsely,
  as a separate and isolated individual? Have you
  abandoned being compassionate, making intimate
  social relations difficult? Does this make the desired
  goals of a happy marriage and family practical
  impossibilities?

~ If you live nicely, but feel left behind compared with
  others, are you a victim of some false view of the
  world? One false view is that of the isolated individual locked in competition with others (American
  individualism) as opposed to being part of a larger
  whole. The perspective of isolation logically cuts off
  compassion and heightens envy.

We can see that the root problems as suggested by
Buddhism are a lack of wisdom and compassion. These
are exemplified in having the wrong views of the self and
the world, improper individualism, extravagance, clutching

at permanence, selfishness, and greed. All of these lead to suffering.

The Five O'Clock Club recommends that you look into your future to set goals that are right for you. To set your goals, write your own obituary (to see how your life would have gone), invent your ideal job, decide what you would do if you had a million dollars (and do it anyway), and write your Forty-Year Vision® (see the Appendix on how to create this vision). The above discussion should help you to do these exercises, since all of us have happiness and the overcoming of suffering as major goals. To sum up, analyze your goals (desires) for their wisdom and compassion to be sure that they will bring you happiness and not suffering. Even this small glimpse at Eastern thinking can challenge us Westerners in varied and positive ways.

What could I say to you that would be of value, except that perhaps you seek too much, that as a result of your seeking you cannot find.

Hermann Hesse

In the depth of winter, I finally learned that there was within me an invincible summer.

Albert Camus

🪶🪶🪶 Group Discussion Questions

• Discuss the common complaints of people who are unhappy in their work. Can you add more?

• Examine the Buddha's framework for dealing with these and analyze critically. 🪶🪶🪶

5

Humility and Success

My List of Virtues contain'd at first but twelve:
But a Quaker Friend having kindly inform'd me that I was
generally thought proud; that my Pride show'd itself frequently
in Conversation; that I was not content with being in the right
when discussing any Point, but was overbearing & rather
insolent; of which he convinc'd me by mentioning several
Instances; I determined endeavoring to cure myself if I could of
this Vice or Folly amoung the rest, and I added Humility to
my List, giving an extensive Meaning to the Word.

Benjamin Franklin

*B*enjamin Franklin, printer, author, diplomat, philosopher, businessman, and scientist, saw fit to make humility his thirteenth virtue (his list: temperance, silence, order, resolution, frugality, industry, sincerity, justice, moderation, cleanliness, tranquility, chastity, and humility).

He concluded that to be humble to one's superiors is our duty, to equals is courtesy, and to inferiors is nobility.

Certainly, Franklin saw business applications in this virtue, but does humility have any currency today? If by humility we mean having a poor image of oneself, and failing to present a positive assessment of one's background in interviews and résumés, then, on a practical basis, the answer is no. And it would be just as hard to reconcile it with The Five O'Clock Club's methodology! Fortunately, that is neither what Franklin nor what others mean by humility.

A good definition of humility is: *to have a proper and not egotistical view about oneself and others.* Andrew Grove, a founder of Intel and author of, *Only the Paranoid Survive,* argues that in business and career planning one ought to be humble to the point of paranoia about market developments. His basic point is well taken, but perhaps we can replace paranoia with other (happier) traits that keep one agile, in touch with the economy and responsive to the market.

Successful people are generally highly sociable. They are able to listen, learn, charm, network, be genuine, make agreements and diffuse difficult social situations. For example, at The Club, people are likely to be long-time members of their professional associations; our best and most senior Five O'Clock Club Coaches are usually the most frequent attendees at our professional Guild meetings.

♪♪♪ **Question(s) to consider**: Are you able to listen, learn, be genuine and diffuse difficult social situations? What can you do to improve in any of these areas? *♪*

Of course, we can think of highly successful people in business and government who we could not call "humble." But we do not know if all ends well with them; and it is likely that such gifted individuals succeed in spite of their arrogance (not because of it).

Duty, courtesy, even nobility, can be characteristics of highly successful people.

Starting around June 2001, there was a period of heavy layoffs. Even in a strong job market—and this is the best it's been since World War II—we can hardly overstate the importance of vigilance in pursuing positive character traits.

Duty, courtesy, even nobility, can be characteristics of highly successful people. The meek, as is often said, may inherit the earth for a number of reasons—the willingness of others to cooperate with them surely being one of the most significant of the reasons! The table below summarizes humility in practice.

Humility in Practice

Character Impact	Manifestation
Insight into one's own need to learn.	• Join professional associations; follow industry trends. • Take classes; read books; subscribe to journals.
Ability to see other perspectives.	• Success at negotiation. • Problem-resolution skills (with clients/colleagues). • DUTY: able to take directions from superiors. • COURTESY: able to be collaborative with peers. • NOBILITY: able to give directions to subordinates in ways that elicit cooperation.
Ability for self-examination and critique.	• Keep careful records to critique and improve one's own work (so others always needn't do the critiquing!). Higher quality work is the consequence.
Pleasant demeanor.	• Nice to be around. Create an atmosphere in which people want to work and produce. Employers love this.
Prudence.	• Not taking unacceptable risks; looking before leaping when making executive decisions. • Compliance with laws and customs.

🖋🖋🖋 **Question(s) to consider**: How often do I think about myself? About others? 🖋

If I have seen further than others, it is by standing upon the shoulders of giants.

Isaac Newton

◌◌◌ Group Discussion Questions

• What is humility as used in this chapter, and how does it differ from the common meaning of the word today?

• Look at the table of "Humility in Practice." Discuss what is there and add your own insights, ideas, and applications of humility. ◌◌◌

6

Compassion

We may have uneasy feelings for seeing a creature in distress without compassion; for we have not compassion unless we wish to relieve them.

Samuel Johnson

When we have a job, we spend most of our waking hours in the workplace, and so our virtues must show there if they are going to show anywhere. The workplace can be a dramatic venue to show compassion if you think about it! It is where hopes rise and fall, reputations are formed, fortunes are made and lost, people develop or squander their talents, systems help or oppress people, colleagues are treated justly or unjustly, and so much more. What an arena for compassion to be championed or stifled in! In other words, the workplace is a setting to show whether or not we have compassion. And it is a choice for most of us. For a select few (the Dalai Lama or the Pope come to mind), compassion is a way of life and is not reserved for special cases or situations.

> 🖉🖉🖉 **Question(s) to consider**: How often do you go out of your way to help someone else? Often? Sometimes? Rarely? Do you look at situations by putting yourself in someone else's shoes? 🖉

Perhaps we don't see as much compassion in the workplace as we might like to because the spirit of competition is so highly prized in our market economy. Products compete for consumer attention, businesses compete for market share, and employees compete for promotions and wage increases. Indeed, we often assume that corporate or personal survival is at stake if we fail to beat the competition.

How can compassion coexist with competition? To answer this question, let's begin by looking at some of the definitions of compassion found in dictionaries:

1. Deep awareness of the suffering of another coupled with the wish to relieve it.

2. A deep awareness of and sympathy for another's suffering; the humane quality of understanding the suffering of others and wanting to do something about it.

So compassion is not incompatible with a moderate sense of competition at the workplace. Two things in particular are important, based on the definition of compassion: (1) awareness and sympathy for another; and (2) doing something about his/her distress, suffering, or misfortune. Anyone who is moved by the needs of others, but doesn't do anything to bring relief, is not compassionate.

Bear in mind: We are not only competitors; we are also colleagues. It's not only realistic, but also necessary for a spirit of compassion to prevail among colleagues. Older, experienced workers show compassion when they mentor new hires until they are comfortable in their new positions. A well-run business requires people and departments to collaborate. Careers and lives can be set back or ruined by cutthroat tactics that lack compassion.

Businesses also show compassion when they donate funds or employee time to charities—and, indeed, thousands of charities benefit from corporate giving. This creates a corporate culture (or character) that makes for a more pleasant world.

In the new economy, businesses often show an active concern for the welfare of other businesses. The Five O'Clock Club has many partners, including the American Management Association, and FutureStep/Korn Ferry, among others. When these do well and prosper, The Club is helped, too. We wish them well and help to promote them.

What is the alternative to compassion? It is competition run wild without boundaries. People would either cease caring for others or stop acting based on caring. Serious damage would be done, given the importance of economic life for all of us. His Holiness The Dalai Lama points out how we all depend on each other to live; some of us grow crops, some make our clothes, some build our homes, some teach our children, and on and on. Without others, our society as it is could not exist.

To sum up, in the often-dramatic world of the workplace, compassion brings us to sympathize with others and actively intervene and help when we see suffering. This not only does much to determine our character (we have to live with ourselves!), but it also creates a constructive environment in which we spend so many of our waking hours.

This is not a matter for theorizing. It's a matter of common sense. There is no denying that consideration of others is worthwhile. There is no denying that our happiness is totally woven in with the happiness of others. There is no denying that if society suffers, we suffer. And there is no denying that the more our hearts and minds are afflicted with ill will, the more miserable we become.

*Compassion is what makes our lives meaningful.
It is the source of all lasting happiness and joy. And it is the
foundation of a good heart, the heart of one who acts out of
a desire to help others. Through kindness, through affection,
through honesty, through truth and justice toward all others
we ensure our own benefit. Thus we can reject everything else:
religion, ideology, all received wisdom. But we cannot escape
the necessity of love and compassion.*

His Holiness The Dalai Lama, *Ethics for the New Millennium*

*True compassion is more than throwing a coin to a beggar.
It demands of our humanity that if we live in a society
that produces beggars,
we are morally commanded to restructure that society.*

Rev. Martin Luther King, Jr.

☙☙☙ Group Discussion Questions

• Is compassion incompatible with a sense of competition at the workplace or in our private lives? State why or why not.

• How can compassion create a constructive environment?
☙☙☙

7

Hope! What Is It? What Good Is It? Who Needs It?

What Is It?

> *Hope is a waking dream.*
>
> Aristotle, 4th century, B.C.

or Aristotle, hope is more than just a happy dream; it is a dream coming into being, or waking. *Webster's Unabridged Dictionary* defines hope as a noun and verb in several ways:

1. The feeling that what is wanted can be had or that events will turn out for the best.

2. The grounds for such a feeling; a person or thing in which expectations are centered.

3. To look forward to with desire and reasonable confidence.

4. To believe, desire, or trust.

5. *Archaic*. To place trust, rely in.

Now, consider hope as a character trait, namely, the habit of looking with reasonable confidence and favorable expectations toward the future. As such, it is a virtue (a strength of character) to be encouraged along with other virtues.

What Good Is It?

> *Hope is the best possession. None are completely wretched but those who are without hope.*
>
> William Hazlitt (1823)

Hope is very useful! In her book, *Targeting a Great Career*, Kate Wendleton quotes Dr. Charles Snyder, a professor at the University of Kansas. He claims his research shows that "Hope has proven a powerful predictor of outcome in every study we've done so far. . . All the skills to solve a problem won't help if you don't have the willpower to do it."

Someone with hope is productive toward his or her goals. Hope is future-oriented and the future is seen as largely under our control. Hope, therefore, is a virtue by which we take responsibility for the future. Our goals are not beyond us; they are only ahead of us. The person with hope accepts few things as givens, even if they obstruct the achievement of his or her goals.

Virtues typically reinforce one another, and this is also true of hope. A number of virtues are necessary to be hopeful: individuals with hope must be able to accept advice, think positively, be resourceful, and remain flexible. Hope would be stifled without these supporting virtues.

Anyone with true hope is not unrealistic. Legitimate hope isn't self-deception; it doesn't minimize the amount of sacrifice involved; it is not pie-in-the-sky. For example, you can't be hopeful to covet the Nobel Prize in physics if you don't have a physics degree! Even here, however, we must be careful: Bill Gates became the richest man and among the most accomplished in this country after dropping out of college!

What happens when there is no hope? People without hope are pessimistic, less productive, despondent about the future, irresponsible, and unsuccessful. These traits destroy a career.

> *✎✎✎* **Question(s) to consider**: Do you think that those with hope succeed more and suffer less? If you are lacking hope, how can you acquire this virtue? *✎*

Who Needs It?

True hope is swift and flies with swallow's wings;
Kings it makes gods, and meaner creatures, kings.

Shakespeare

Of course, all of us need hope. This side of death we have a future, and we want it to be a good one. So we should all work to make our futures excellent.

However, there are some for whom hope is particularly important. For example, people who are crucial in the lives of others should spread hope because of their special role. In particular, this means doctors, the clergy, lawyers and others in high-impact professions. Such people often have the power to either build up or crush hope in others. The doctor, for example, can inspire hope in the patient, which helps not only because of his/her being optimistic, but also inspires adhering to a medication regime and working hard for one's own recovery. This is not a false hope, no matter how severe the diagnosis. Something can always be done for health or comfort, or simply making the best of the remaining time.

Beyond the professions, the entrepreneur definitely must be hopeful for his/her own sake. This industrious individual invests his or her time, money, credibility, and his very survival in a vision for his own business. There is no guarantee of success; there is only a hope of it! In being hopeful, the entrepreneur sees things that are not there; he sees things as they might be. This commitment to hope is not shallow. It involves all that someone has to give (time, money, credibility, energy, and sometimes survival). Indeed, few people have hope that encompasses all of these. Hope in the form of entrepreneurship is the great engine driving capitalism, and is sorely needed in the young market economies around the globe.

But it's not just entrepreneurs, of course, who need hope. Young people facing a professional life of 40 or 50 years need a vision based on hope. And senior-level employees need hope so that the organization thrives and grows. The very act of planning presumes hope. Good planning assumes reasonable hope and having the underlying virtues: a consultative mentality, positive thinking, resourcefulness, and flexibility.

*I have learned two lessons in my life:
first, there are no sufficient literary, psychological,
or historical answers to human tragedy, only moral ones.
Second, just as despair can come to one another only from
other human beings, hope, too, can be given
to one only by other human beings.*

Elie Wiesel

🖋🖋🖋 Group Discussion Questions

- What is hope, and who needs it?
- Why might hope be a predictor of future success?
- Is hope self deception?
- Discuss the importance of hope among the clergy, doctors, lawyers, and others in the professions.

🖋🖋🖋

8

Generosity in Deed:
The Virtue of Thrift

To be thrifty is to be happy and generous!
Avoid stinginess and extravagance.

Aristotle

t's by being virtuous that we achieve genuine happiness— our full flourishing. The moral virtue of thrift can be considered paramount here.

A virtue is the habit of doing the right thing at the right time,
toward the right people, for the right reason,
and in the right manner.

Aristotle

A good way to begin discussing thrift is by considering the beliefs of the greatest of all philosophers, Aristotle. In Book Two of his *Nicomachean Ethics*, a virtue is defined as the habit of doing the right thing, at the right time, toward the right people, for the right reason, and in the right manner. Aristotle viewed the median as the best course, the course that is a mark of virtue. Think of it as navigating a boat down a river while trying to avoid hitting the bank on either side. The best course is the median course.

When I was a professor, I used to tell my students that philosophy was about life. We can see this in the following table of moral virtues. Aristotle gives us delightful examples of what he means by median, and here are several:

Aristotle considers both deficiencies and the excesses as vices. He also gives some good practical advice. We should make a conscious effort to lean toward the extreme to which we are least prone. For example, if we are stingy, we should consciously lean toward extravagance in the hopes of approaching the median. In this case, the median is being generous.

If we tend to be stingy, we should consciously lean toward extravagance and hope to approach being generous.

Which brings us to a discussion of thrift, or the giving and taking of money. The ideal is to be generous, without being stingy or extravagant. So, if we are basically stingy, we should lean toward being extravagant; if we are extravagant, we should try to be somewhat stingy. We do this in the hopes of hitting the mean of generosity.

> 🖉🖉🖉 **Question(s) to consider**: How much credit card debt do you carry? How much do you regularly contribute to charity? Which of these gets most of your attention? 🖉

Therefore, to be thrifty does not exclude being generous, but rather, encompasses it. Virtuous people help the needy, care for their children, assist their parents in old age, and especially show a concern for those with whom they share a special relationship. This is what it means to have a generous soul.

Thrift stems from the same root as the verb "to thrive." So, there is no question of living a miserable existence just to give all to others, or hoarding to the extent of living in poverty. The thrifty person also is a thriving person! There is a reasonable concern (a middle way) for the present, as well as for the future.

Thus, being thrifty is not being stingy. Thrifty people show a rightful concern for their own future and financial stability, and mind the needs of others. In other words, moths don't fly out of the wallet when it's time to pay bills and reach out to help others. Hoarding is not so much a concern today as it was after World War II when goods were extremely scarce, making practicing thrift difficult.

A thrifty person has a generous soul.

Finally, the thrifty person is not extravagant. An extravagant person engages in conspicuous consumption (owning things for the sake of being envied by others), buys in excess, and may not plan for his/her financial future. Extravagance is a particular vice of American culture. Indeed, conspicuous consumption is a cultural plague, since it does not recognize fully the needs of others (other nations included), and endangers the environment by creating mountains of trash. We consume at a rate that endangers future generations.

We also see people racking up credit card debt, neglecting to invest in IRAs, and refinancing their homes to have cash to spend now—at the cost of future retirement, all to have more things now.

> 🌿🌿🌿 **Question(s) to consider**: Again on a scale of 1 to 10, 1 being something that you do purely for pleasure, and 10 being something you do for virtue/goodness (helping others, taking courses to acquire new skills, etc.) how do you rank yourself? 🌿

And as we're straddling from one deal to the next, who's got his eye on the planet, as the air thickens, the water sours, and even the bees' honey takes on the metallic taste of radioactivity? And it just keeps coming, faster and faster. There's no chance to think, to prepare; it's buy futures, sell futures, when there is no future!

From the movie, "The Devil's Advocate"

You want to be happy? Do you want to achieve your full flourishing? Then be thrifty (generous) as much as you can in the sense outlined here. Aristotle's practical advice is to aim for your opposite extreme in hopes of hitting the median.

**Extravagance is a particular vice
of American culture.**

Study Questions:

- Are you stingy or extravagant?
- Are you living within your means?
- Are you saving for retirement and for a rainy day?
- Do you have an IRA?
- Are you generous toward the poor?
- Do you care for your parents, including financially?
- Is your credit card debt beyond your means to cope with it?
- Do you consider the environment when you purchase a car, a house, and so on?
- Do you have your eye on the planet?
- Do you engage in conspicuous consumption?
- Do you make an effort to lean toward the other extreme, that is, the one to which you do not naturally lean, in hopes of hitting the median?

Aristotle's Table of Moral Values

Matters of:	Deficiency	Virtue (The Median)	Excess
Fear/Confidence	Cowardly	Courageous	Reckless
Pleasure/Pain	Insensitive	Self-controlling	Self-indulging
Giving/Taking Money	Stingy	Generous	Extravagant
Honor/Dishonor	Small-minded	High-minded	Vain
Anger	Apathetic	Gentle	Short-tempered
Truth	Self-deprecating	Truthful	Boastful
Amusement	Boorish	Witty	Buffoonish!
Pleasantness	Grouchy	Friendly	Obsequious

🪶🪶🪶 Group Discussion Questions

- What is a moral virtue?
- Discuss all study questions listed in this chapter. 🪶🪶🪶

9

The Search for Truth— or Not: The Problem with Secularism

Once religion is disestablished, it tends to become part of the "private sphere," and privatization is part of the story of American religion. Yet religion, and certainly biblical religion, is concerned with the whole of life—with social, economic, and political matters as well as with private and personal ones.

Robert N. Bellah et al., *Habits of the Heart*

How should you think about your work life? What are you thinking when you do your Seven Stories Exercise® and your Forty-Year Vision®? (These exercises are found in the Appendix.) How do you set your priorities? How do you rank them? How do you deal with conflicting priorities? Practical answers to such questions depend not only on your worldview, but also on nothing less than the U.S. Constitution and current social trends.

A Worldview

In our pluralistic society, a worldview is a matter of choice; society is secular in the way that there is no one established philosophy or religion, and so we are free to choose. Christians, Jews, and Muslims are free to follow the God of Abraham; Buddhists seek enlightenment; and so forth. Those living by a philosophy may follow Marxism, to name one example, which claims that all history is that of class struggle; hence, it is crucial to advance the cause of the proletariat (worker). Marxism as a philosophy has been the choice of many in this and especially the previous century.

So we are free to discover what is actually real and valuable. This is what the U.S. Constitution guarantees. The disestablishment clause protects and serves the free exercise of religion:

Amendment 1

Congress shall make no law respecting an establishment of religion, or prohibiting the free exercise thereof; or abridging the freedom of speech, or of the press; or the right of the people peaceably to assemble, and to petition the Government for a redress of grievances.

This is all great, and it is required by our basic human dignity. What is disturbing, however, is a much harder brand of secularism that has grown rapidly in popularity.

Hard Secularism

There is a type of secularism today not envisioned by the constitutional writers. Let us call it "hard secularism." This type of secularism goes beyond the freedom to choose a religion or the freedom to choose a philosophy to follow. Hard secularism says that there is nothing inherently real. And there is nothing inherently valuable! Consequently, there is no search for reality and value, no search for truth, or for beauty and genuine goodness, since these do not exist. What generally remains is the simple search for pleasure and various forms of gratification. This is a life of jumping from one buzz to another to push back boredom and a sense of emptiness. Since nothing tells people where they fit in as unique human beings, young people frequently adopt pseudo differences such as green hair, rings in their noses or tongues, and more. The table below shows a comparison of these two worldviews:

In a nutshell, hard secularism uses the disestablishment clause not to protect our right to pursue the truth and value as we see fit, but to deny the existence of truth and value.

The Five O'Clock Club methodologies can, of course, accommodate even hard secularism. The benefits, though, of the original secularism (pluralism) as envisioned by the framers of the Constitution are many.

Pluralist Position

A pluralist believes that there are some things that are inherently real and valuable. To have good character (i.e., to possess the traditional virtues of courage, justice, wisdom, and prudence) is a good thing to have to lead a good life. Who is really genuinely happy and content being cowardly, unjust, foolish, and imprudent? *Therefore, the theologians and philosophers of the past have much to teach us about human existence, because there is objectively much to learn.* The United Nations also *presumes the pluralist position* when it defends "human dignity" as it so often has. In fact, ignoring hard secular arguments, the United Nations sends military personnel into various countries precisely to defend human life and well-being! Similarly, highly respected groups, such as Amnesty International, exist to protect human dignity by fighting against torture and the indecent treatment of people by governments.

> 🖉🖉🖉 **Question(s) to consider**: Do you regularly pursue goals that are worthwhile and protect human dignity? For example, do you do anything to help the working poor (donate clothing, food, money) or the poor in places like Africa? How important are these goals in your life? 🖉

The original secular viewpoint allows people to discover things about life that they take to be real and valuable. It becomes possible to synthesize different truths and values. This can lead to personality integration—a good thing for psychiatric health. This was the belief of the great psychologist Karl Jung (1875–1961) who also claimed that the loss of religious belief often lead to psychiatric illness. People should not only have goals, but they also should have *worthy* goals, since, as the pluralist says, some goals are indeed better and more authentically in line with human life and dignity than others.

How should you think about your work life, your Seven Stories Exercise®, your Forty-Year Vision®? How do you set and rank your priorities? Our Constitution and ethos today allow wide leeway. Follow the original framers of the Constitution. Use your freedom to pick some *authentic* way of being, to have some *worthy* goals, and some *insightful* philosophy or a religion by which to *guide your life*. This helps to bring life into a focus and sets you up for a sense of accomplishment in later years.

Worldview	Definition	Consequence
Original secularism (pluralist)	The person is free to discover what is actually real and valuable about life.	Reality and value may be discovered in and through a world religion, or perhaps some philosophy (Plato, Marx, etc.). Truth and value generally achieve some sort of synthesis that is satisfying to the person's mind and heart.
Hard secularism	There is nothing inherently real and nothing inherently valuable about life.	The individual lives life according to arbitrary wants and desires. He or she follows values chosen idiosyncratically. Frequent result is hedonism, nihilism, complete relativism about values, and materialism.

✍✍✍ Group Discussion Questions

• What is meant by "hard secularism," and how does it use the disestablishment clause of the constitution?

• Contrast hard secularism with pluralism as world views. Do you agree with the table presented in this chapter? ✍✍✍

10

Cheated by Writing a Blank Check!—To Science

There is a danger that in his excessive confidence in modern invention man may give up the search for higher values.

Austin Flannery, O.P.

There are two worldviews: traditional and modern. The traditional one still has much to offer those of us who want to find happiness in life. A traditional worldview is the one that prevailed until the rise of *modern science*. The modern worldview followed this.

Of course, modern science has much to offer. Modern science, along with technology, has given us unprecedented control over nature and a high living standard. We can only admire the achievements of today's scientists. Unfortunately, we have forgotten that there are questions that science can't answer. Science can tell us, for example, something about *how* the universe came into being and developed, but it can't tell us *why*. It can't tell what might exist beyond material realities, nor can it answer questions of purpose, meaning, and value. In short, we have a need to know many things that science can't answer.

> 🖉🖉🖉 **Question(s) to consider**: Do you ever think about the *why* of things—what is the purpose of life? *Your* life? Are your thoughts on the latest laptop, car, drug? Is there a meaning to your life, or is this not an important question to you? 🖉

Religion goes beyond the material focus of science when it concerns the question of spirit. People long to know their place in reality; we long to know, "Why am I here?" and "What is important for me to do?" among other fundamental questions. Science clearly does not even claim to be able to answer such questions. But today, these longings are covered up because people typically refuse to accept knowledge from sources other than science with its focus on the material world and its mathematical methods. We are cheated because we have written science a blank check; the modern scientific worldview has suffocated many deep longings that we have.

Traditional worldviews provided such knowledge. The Christian worldview, for example, concerns itself with creation, sin, redemption, God, and the nature and destiny of humankind. Islam, Judaism, Buddhism, Hinduism, and other ancient religions provide their version of this important type of knowledge. While each of these traditions has its own distinct teachings, it is remarkable how much they agree on many fundamental questions.

Of course, no one wants to give up the fruits of modern science and technology. We enjoy a standard of living (at least in the West) previously unknown, and we intend to keep it! If only our culture had adopted a stance like this:

We all welcome the knowledge provided to us by science and its mathematical methods. We welcome the power this gives us, when combined with technology, to raise living standards so that we may lead long lives in dignity and relatively free of disease. At the same time, we recognize that science only answers a limited set of questions. We can't ignore questions that are important to us and that concern matters of the spirit, human life, life after death, and so on. We still need sources of genuine knowledge—which include religion, liberal education, the humanities, and philosophy.

(Source Unknown)

Unfortunately, what has happened instead was the downplaying or *loss* of questions that science can't answer. Nothing in the modern era is really considered true unless verified by science. For this reason, religion, art, the humanities, and a liberal education are all dismissed as too traditional. They aren't considered to be reliable sources of knowledge. Unfortunately, the deepest questions about human existence can only be answered by them.

At the present, the common person holds science in more esteem than do scientists who recognize this discipline's limitations. What we should do is cancel that blank check. Let us search for answers to the deepest human longings in the right places.

How on earth are you ever going to explain in terms of chemistry and physics so important a biological phenomenon as first love?

Albert Einstein

✎✎✎ Group Discussion Questions

• Modern science has raised the standard of living for humankind. Are there any areas or questions which it can not answer?

• Does the modern scientific view have any shortcomings?

✎✎✎

11

What Is America all About?
A Perspective from
"America the Beautiful"

The author of this hymn to our country, Katharine Lee Bates, was born at Falmouth, Massachusetts, on August 12, 1859, the daughter of the Congregational Church pastor. The family moved to Wellesley when she was young and she graduated from high school there, and from Wellesley College in 1874. She was a professor of English at the college until 1925.

Surprised by the song's immediate and lasting success, she wrote: "That the hymn has gained, in these 20-odd years, such a hold as it has upon our people, is clearly due to the fact that Americans are at heart idealists, with a fundamental faith in human brotherhood." The text was written in 1893 and had its final revision in 1913. The hymn offers a profound snapshot of how Americans understood themselves and their country during the last century.

Let's look at a few key verses:

> *... God shed his grace on thee*
> *And crown thy good*
> *with brotherhood...*

The text asks for God's grace so that "good" (read "common good") includes brotherhood. In other words, the common good—that which is in the interests of all people—does not just include freedom, and/or equality, as they are popularly understood today. The common good must include brotherhood. This is a strong challenge to much contemporary thinking that allows for excessive individualism and the attitude of the me generation. Another verse is:

> *God mend thine every flaw,*
> *Confirm thy soul in self-control,*
> *Thy liberty in law!*

The dictionary describes "self-control" as restraint of one's actions, feelings, and so on. To exercise self-control is to deny one part of the self in favor of another. Self-control puts the intellect and wisdom ahead of one's feelings and emotions. It keeps us from being slaves to our momentary passions.

But being slaves to our momentary passions is precisely what some parts of American culture today expect and encourage. For example, advertisers want us to feel that we should buy their products *now* for various emotional reasons. Television commercials want us to yield to impulse. Through music and images of glamorous people and products, they promise excitement and happiness—if only we buy the advertised products right away. The movies are full of uncontrolled sex and violence. Uncontrolled sex promises happiness; uncontrolled violence brings release through the destruction of the bad guy. But as our hymn says, uncontrolled behaviors don't really bring much hope and happiness to the soul.

To confirm liberty in law seems at first to be a paradox. Aren't they opposites? If something is illegal and therefore not permitted, how does it confirm liberty? There are two common understandings of liberty, however. In fact, one is a misunderstanding of liberty, because it holds that liberty exists in the absence of law and restraint. The second understanding makes more sense, since it sees the positive connection between liberty and law. Good laws can actually enhance liberty and make freedom possible in daily life.

For example, our liberty to drive is protected by stop signs, traffic lights, speed limits, and other rules (laws) that regulate the driver's behavior behind the wheel, as well as the behavior of pedestrians. Otherwise, it would be dangerous to drive and we would not feel free to do much driving—especially with loved ones in the car. So good laws promote liberty, when we consider that our actions must be coordinated with the actions of others. Thus, "Confirm . . . Thy liberty in law" makes perfect sense, because true liberty is not license.

▱ ▱ ▱ **Question(s) to consider**: Do you value liberty, the right to do anything you want without regard to your impact on others? Do you do things because you can get away with it or do you restrain yourself for the good of others? For example, do you drive well above the speed limit when you can get away with it? Do you shoplift? Under-tip service workers? *▱*

In addition to liberty and law, Bates concerns herself with selfishness:

> *. . . God shed his grace on thee*
> *Till selfish gain no longer stain*
> *The banner of the free!*

The hymn implores God's grace to fight selfishness. Being selfish is being committed to oneself, concerned mainly with one's own well being, interests, benefits, etc., without regard for our brothers and sisters. Selfishness is a stain upon the banner of the free. Bates understood that, "Americans are at heart idealists, with a fundamental faith in human brotherhood." So, in summation, liberty and equality amount to very little without brotherhood.

"America the Beautiful"

(1913 revision, Selected verses)

O beautiful for spacious skies,
For amber waves of grain,
For purple mountain majesties
Above the fruited plain!
America! America!
God shed his grace on thee
And crown thy good with brotherhood
From sea to shining sea!

O beautiful for pilgrim feet
Whose stern, impassioned stress
A thoroughfare for freedom beat
Across the wilderness!
America! America!
God mend thine every flaw,
Confirm thy soul in self-control,
Thy liberty in law!

O beautiful for glory-tale
Of liberating strife
When once and twice,

For man's avail
Men lavished precious life!
America! America!
God shed his grace on thee
Till selfish gain no longer stain
The banner of the free!

✐✐✐ Group Discussion Questions

• What does the common good include besides freedom and equality?

• Is it self contradictory to say "confirm liberty in law?"
✐✐✐

12

How to Make Ethical Decisions in Business

It's not hard to make decisions
when you know what your values are.

Roy Disney, American Film Writer,
Producer, Nephew of Walt Disney

Because business activity is human activity, it can be evaluated
from the moral point of view, just as any other human activity
can be so evaluated. The relationship of business to morality
goes even deeper than this. Business, like most other
social activities, presupposes a background of
morality and would be impossible without it.

Richard T. De George, *Business Ethics*,
Fifth Edition, Prentice Hall, New Jersey, 1999.

usiness leaders make ethical decisions every day. What if we were to assume that, "Let your conscience be your guide," is the simple tenet that most people follow when they grapple with ethical issues in organizations? It's actually far more complex than that—usually because the situations and issues in the workplace are complex.

"Let your conscience be your guide," does not provide the necessary guidance.

For example, what should hiring managers do about questions of diversity, quotas, and affirmative action? How should a CEO go about deciding how much to spend to reduce air and water pollution caused by her company? When is advertising a forceful presentation of a product's strengths, and when does it claim too much and betray the public's trust? How should a reduction in workforce be carried out, and how does the firm determine the right amounts for severance, career counseling (outplacement), and benefits coverage for those being terminated?

> ✐✐✐ **Question(s) to consider**: When you make business decisions at work, how often do you consider ethics a part of them? Or are you only thinking about reaching a goal or implementing a plan? Always, sometimes, rarely or never? ✐

"Let your conscience be your guide," falls far short of providing the necessary guidance in such matters. There are, in fact, *concrete methods for ethical reasoning*. Indeed, historically, there are several approaches that people have used.

Examining these can be fascinating, as well as aid in making ethical decisions in the organization. In the section that follows, we'll cover three of the most highly regarded, with emphasis on Economic Personalism, which is the most helpful and comprehensive (it includes the insights contained in the first two).

Let's look at the inspirational Johnson & Johnson Tylenol case to help us examine ethical reasoning.

To prevent this discussion from sounding too theoretical, the best approach is presenting a case study, involving real people in a life-and-death situation—literally. Let's look at the inspirational Johnson & Johnson Tylenol case. It provides a good example for analyzing the methods used to reason ethically.

On September 30, 1982, three people in the Chicago area died from cyanide introduced into Extra-Strength Tylenol capsules. The link between the deaths and the tainted capsules was made with remarkable speed, and authorities notified Johnson & Johnson. As the number of deaths grew—the final total was seven—the firm faced a crisis and, indeed, potential disaster. Tylenol, a leading pain-reliever, was Johnson & Johnson's single largest brand, accounting for almost 18 percent of the corporation's income.

The executives involved in deciding how to respond did not know:

· Had the cyanide been put in the Tylenol capsules during the manufacturing process or afterwards?

- Were the deaths that had already been reported just the first of a large number?
- Would the deaths be limited to the Chicago area?

The U.S. Food and Drug Administration had issued a warning not to take Tylenol, but the government had not ordered the company to take any specific action. Perhaps the deaths would be local, and there would be no more than seven. Perhaps the authorities would not demand a recall. Perhaps a temporary cessation of sales until the source of the contamination was determined could prevent more harm to the public.

Against all these unknowns, the Johnson & Johnson executives had to weigh several certainties:

- A recall would involve a loss of up to $100 million.
- The loss was not covered by insurance.
- News of a recall could so damage the product that Tylenol might never be able to regain public confidence and its 37 percent of market share.
- The news and loss would surely result in a dramatic drop in the company's stock (it did, in fact, go down 15 percent in the first week of October).
- The competition in the analgesic market was fierce. Competitors would try to make Tylenol's loss their gain.

**Public welfare and the company's reputation were both
protected by ethical decision-making.**

These were certainties; the rest was guesswork and specu-
lation. But, being unwilling to expose consumers to further
risk—and in making a decision that put it in the Ethics Hall
of Fame—Johnson & Johnson ordered a recall of all Tylenol
bottles. In the long run, public welfare and the company's
reputation were both protected by ethical decision-making.

The Tylenol case obviously presents a major example of
ethical reasoning. But ethical issues, large and small, occur
every day. Business leaders need methods for dealing with
them and arriving at reasonable decisions. There are three
major approaches in ethics that have been fashioned by philosophers and theologians, *which are applied every day by
many leaders who may never have read their works.*

There are three major approaches to ethical decision-
making.

Approach One: Universal Obligation

One way to look at it is this: *moral rules derive from
our rights and duties toward one another.* The thinker most
closely connected with this approach is the great philosopher
Immanuel Kant (1724–1804), as expressed in his *Groundwork*

of the Metaphysic of Morals. For Kant, actions are not good or bad based on the purposes for which we act. Rather than considering purposes, we should ask if the basis of our action could become a "universal law" for all moral actors in similar circumstances. If it is wrong for any company to sell a potentially defective product, it is wrong for Johnson & Johnson to do so—despite the considerable cost of a recall. The focus is on motivation, not on the consequences of an action. Further, since all human beings share this ability to reason about moral actions, Kant believed that no one must ever be treated purely as a means, but, rather, as an end in himself. We cannot use others purely for some benefit to ourselves.

This rule would prohibit seeing the consumer purely as a means to corporate profit—as could have been done in the Tylenol case (but was not). Johnson & Johnson correctly recognized its duty to consumer welfare. However, the Kantian approach fails to consider the ends of an action. Indeed, it is often said, "The way to hell is paved with good intentions." Morality should, however, consider the consequences (not just the motives) of an action on the actual human beings who are impacted.

Universal Obligation:
Never use others purely for some benefit to ourselves.

A Modern Understanding of Universal Obligation

One of the foremost philosophers of the twentieth century, John Rawls, takes a position very similar to Kant. Now Professor Emeritus at Harvard, in 1971 Rawls first published *A Theory of Justice.* He argued that people choose proper rules when they are forced to reason impartially. Rawls asks people to reason from what he calls an "original position." People should, in fact, imagine themselves behind a veil of ignorance. That is, they are free, equal, rational, self-interested, but, in the original position, they do not know their place in society. They neither have an idea about how well they will fare in the natural lottery of talents, nor do they know their likes, dislikes, religious beliefs, and so on. They know only the general facts about human society. It is assumed that they have different aims (life plans), but they cannot advance them at the cost of others, since all knowledge is held behind the veil of ignorance. *Ignorance of these things guarantees impartiality in ethical choice.*

According to this method of reasoning (from behind the veil of ignorance), the management and stockholders of Johnson & Johnson would have reasoned impartially, that is, they would never have put the consumer at risk any more than they would have been willing to put themselves at risk. However, the Rawls method has a serious flaw; few of us can reason so abstractly about concrete, everyday moral problems.

This becomes especially clear when Rawls spells out what we must "forget" to reason ethically—our place in society, our talents, likes, dislikes, religious beliefs, and so on. The criticism made about Kant also applies to Rawls. The impact of any moral decision on real people never comes clearly into focus. The failure to consider consequences is resolved in the next approach.

The Consequences Approach:
Take actions that produce the most
good for the most people.

Approach Two: What Is the Impact of What You Do?

There are those, however, who believe that morality is about consequences, not rules and duty. This approach is known as Utilitarianism, and was argued most strongly by John Stuart Mill (1806–1873). According to him, actions are considered morally right if these produce the most good for the most people.

Utilitarianism seeks "The greatest good for the greatest number." Following this code, the decision makers at Johnson & Johnson would have been forced to consider not only the interests of the company, but also those of the public at large. Determining the greatest good for the greatest number requires a cost/benefit analysis to be done for the public, as well as for the organization.

This reasoning method *probably* would have required a product recall. The protection of the millions of Tylenol users is the greater good and outweighs the financial costs to Johnson & Johnson.

But if only a few were to be poisoned, what then? *Unfortunately, utilitarianism would allow large and unfair burdens to be placed on the few (i.e., the risk of death), to the benefit of the greatest number.* This runs against our ethical sensibility. It also says little about what is meant by the greatest "good." This flaw is remedied by the Personalist approach.

Approach Three: Economic Personalism

Personalism has human dignity at its center. Sources such as the United Nations, Christian social thought, and the Dalai Lama support this ethic. According to this approach, ethical reasoning asks, "Which action most leads to the protection and promotion of human dignity?" Of course, how one understands the human person is the key to answering this question.

The preferred approach is, Economic Personalism: Choose the action that most likely leads to the protection and promotion of human dignity.

Aspects of the Person to Consider

Those within the Judeo-Christian tradition believe that all persons were created in the image and likeness of God. This belief is the foundation for protecting and promoting human dignity. Catholic social thought, in particular, latches onto this approach to answer questions of business and economic ethics. (As already indicated, it is not only Jews and Christians who affirm human dignity, but also others—Muslims, philosophers, and still others—who do so for their own reasons and within their own traditions. The reader who is neither Jew nor Christian should be able to find application for all or most of the ideas presented here.)

The following discussion covers the six basic aspects of the human person to consider when making ethical decisions in your everyday worklife using the Economic Personalism approach. After surveying these aspects, we'll look at how they would have affected decision-making in the Tylenol situation. These characteristics, which were presented earlier in this chapter, are now looked at in terms of Economic Personalism. The six are summarized in the table below.

> *◌◌◌* **Question(s) to consider**: So far, has reading this section in any way changed how you would go about making an ethical decision? If so, how? *◌*

Protecting Human Dignity at the Workplace

Characteristics of Human Beings	Definition	Example, Application
1. Spiritual	A person must have "space" to practice spirituality.	Respect and encouragement for various belief systems. Time or days off for religious holidays is important.
2. Social	A person only develops to his/her fullest with others.	Employees should have opportunities to socialize, participate in groups, work in cooperative settings, and join appropriate associations.
3. Material	A person requires food, clothing, shelter, etc., to survive.	Payment of just wages and benefits. Safe and pleasant working conditions.
4. Free and Creative	We all want to move forward professionally, to exercise our creative abilities.	Assignments should assign creative responsibility at the lowest level possible.
5. Fragile	We are all prone to error; have our weaknesses; and failings.	Employees need oversight, second chances, extra training, or re-assignment.
6. Equal	Persons have a basic equality regardless of race, color, creed, etc.	There should not be discrimination on a non-performance basis.

1. **Spiritual.** In Economic Personalism, all things on earth are understood as being ordered to human beings as their center and summit. Indeed, humans are spiritual beings, distinguished from other creatures by their capacity to know and love. In other words, God gives persons their true being, not simply in the sense of existence in time and space, but in the sense of life purpose, meaning, and ethical structure.

   To become truly spiritual, one must have "space" to delve into one's soul. This means that ethical decisions must respect and encourage various belief systems. For example, people need time off from work for religious holidays. It's a company's duty to help a Muslim be a good Muslim, for example, by giving her the space to practice spirituality.

Human beings are distinguished from other creatures by their capacity to know and love.

2. **Communal.** Christians believe that God's being is not solitary, but communal. For example, there is a community of persons, Father, Son, and the Holy Spirit, who all give and receive love. Humans, created in the image and likeness of God, also find their true being in giving and receiving love and in experiencing unity in the midst of difference. Since Economic

Personalism says that a person only develops to his or her fullest with others, it is our ethical responsibility to encourage this. For example, employers can give employees the opportunity to socialize, participate in groups, work in cooperative settings, and join appropriate associations.

3. **Material.** In applying Economic Personalism, we need to consider the material aspect of a person. The basis for this is that God has created persons as body and spirit, and our everyday material processes should serve to reveal the hidden presence of God. Although, realistically speaking, the activities of caring for the body, providing for the needs of family and self, participating in economic life, do involve some repetition and, at times toil, the more striking truth is that during these activities we can discover and recognize the workings and presence of the Creator.

Consider the act of eating. We eat and provide nourishment for the material needs of the body, but we almost always prefer to do this communally. Therefore, the material overlaps with the spiritual. Eating can become almost a spiritual event. Indeed, for Christians, the Eucharist, a meal, is the high point of worship.

Therefore, ethical decision-makers should consider that a person requires food, shelter, and clothing to survive, and so should pay just wages and benefits, as well as provide safe and pleasant working conditions.

**Johnson & Johnson put people before money.
Its executives understood their social responsibility to
protect persons, whose unique value is inestimable.**

4. **Free and Creative.** Economic Personalism also rests upon providing freedom for the individual, because only by exercising our freedom can we turn ourselves toward what is truly good. In our freedom and creativity, we may participate in and contribute to giving and receiving love, involving God and other persons. The more people who are involved, the more giving and receiving of love there is. Thus, an ethical decision-maker at work helps people to move forward professionally, and to exercise their creative abilities.

5. **Fragile.** Of course, a realistic understanding of humans must recognize the significance of our being finite (having limitations), and the toughness and cohesiveness of our moral failings. Due to our limitations, we can never achieve the good that we often desire. We must learn patience, humility, and realism in setting objectives. Refusal to do this rejects our bodily nature. Further, in our freedom we have

all refused to participate as we should in giving and receiving love; the image of God in us all thereby is lessened and distorted.

Since we are all prone to our weaknesses and moral inconsistencies, managers should offer employees compassionate oversight, second chances, extra training, or even reassignment.

❧ ❧ ❧ **Question(s) to consider**: When you make a mistake at work, do you try to cover it up, or do you own up to it? *❧*

6. **Equal.** Human equality here means that all of us are called to know and to love God; all have certain rights and duties with respect to others; and all should have equal opportunity. Such basic equality is the basis to provide all persons (especially the disadvantaged) with the necessary material and nonmaterial support to achieve the ends of human life. A consequence of this is that we must not discriminate based on non-performance.

Back to Johnson & Johnson

It seems that Johnson & Johnson understood its social responsibility to protect persons, whose unique value is inestimable. Human beings were put before things (money in this case). This action was consistent with the protection of human dignity, and, therefore, the recall was a proper exercise of managerial freedom. Given that human beings are morally inconsistent and shortsighted creatures, there could've been the temptation to do otherwise.

Economic Personalism also includes the wisdom shown in the prior methods. Universal obligation (Kant and Rawls) must be respected because of our equal human dignity, and we must consider carefully the ultimate impact (Utilitarianism) on actual human beings when reaching a judgment. However, Economic Personalism far surpasses utilitarianism in defining what we mean by human beings and their innate dignity.

Recognizing its social obligation, Johnson & Johnson acted to protect people on the material level. Because they, too, were fragile and morally inconsistent, the Johnson & Johnson executives could have chosen otherwise.

Spiritually, they maintained our trust. They recognized basic equality by not putting their own good above others. Summing up, they chose the action that most led to the protection and promotion of human dignity.

> ✐✐✐ **Question(s) to consider**: When you purchase a product or service, do you consider how ethical the company is? For example, how do they handle layoffs? How truthful is their advertising? Where are their foreign investments? Are they socially responsible by considering the environmental

impact of what they do, by hiring the less fortunate, including ex-inmates, and by having a positive impact on their local
community? 🖋

**Given our nature as morally inconsistent and
shortsighted creatures, Johnson & Johnson
could have been tempted to do otherwise.**

It is a relief to ethicists and moralists—and a source of
deep satisfaction— that Johnson & Johnson fared so well in
the long run in the wake of its highly ethical actions. We see
that ethical behavior can be consistent with surviving and
making money.

*The dilemma of our age is the combination of unprecedented
material progress and systematic spiritual decline. The
decline in public and private morality can be witnessed in the
marketplace as well as the forums of international diplomacy.
In the past, a man's honor and reputation were his most
valuable assets. Business agreements were made with a
handshake. Today one might be well advised to
check the "bottom line" and read the "small print."*

King Hussein (1935–1999), Commencement Forum speech,
graduation of his son Prince Feisal, Brown University, May 1985

✎✎✎ Group Discussion Questions

• Is the maxim "Let conscience be your guide" sufficient to provide ethical direction in today's complex world?

• What makes Johnson & Johnson a model for corporate ethical behavior?

• Optional Question: compare and contrast the ethical theories of Kant, Rawls, and Mill.

• What is economic Personalism? Can you add ideas to the table on "Protecting Human Dignity in the Workplace?

• What course of ethical direction does Personalism recommend for Johnson & Johnson? ✎✎✎

13

Good Ethics Is Serious Business: Objections and Answers

Cowards can never be moral.

Gandhi (1869–1948)

We now know that the 1990s boom included much wrongdoing. Given the scandals around Enron, Global Crossing, WorldCom, Arthur Anderson, and other major companies, it is not surprising that the media has reported a boom in ethics education not seen before in corporate life. Business schools, for example, are capitalizing on this: New York University has recently come up with an $1,850 two-day course for board members aimed at avoiding ethical lapses and law suits. The number of ethics compliance officers in corporations jumped from 12, ten years earlier, to over 800 in 2005. Bad ethics can literally be the undoing of the proudest of corporations. A staggering thought indeed.

Even more staggering is the negative impact on the *national economy* these events are believed to have had.

But, of course, there are persistent and important objections to these new courses and trainings that revolve around the following four points:

Objections to Ethics Training

1. *Lawsuits* are all we do and should care about.

2. *Political correctness* to do the right thing is too strong to overcome.

3. *Youth* is the only time possible for ethical formation.

4. *Expertise* is lacking when and where it counts.

Let's discuss these in order, since they are the dominant arguments given *why* ethical training is not important today.

Some argue that corporations do not care about something as sublime as "ethics," but only want compliance with the *law*. This may be true, but it is a terrible mistake. Walking a narrow legal tightrope inevitably results in a few falls—perhaps a fall far enough to bring down the company. Laws are also often ambiguous and it is better to be on the safe side so as not to endanger the entire company.

In our society, *political correctness* often favors ethics. It is politically correct not to harm the environment, to hire with diversity in mind, and so forth. However, there are also corrupt corporate cultures in which so-called "political correctness" can sanction misdeeds. Again, we need some sort of ethical standard and training from the *outside*.

Now some argue that only in *youth* do we learn ethics. This is pure, unadulterated nonsense! Until the day we die, we learn about how correctly to treat other people, we come to a better understanding of principles that guide us, we come better to comprehend moral norms, and so forth. We would not want to be stuck with an eight year-old's understanding of ethics any more than we would want to be stuck with an eight year-old's understanding of reading, writing, and arithmetic! This is a contemptible excuse to escape ethical demands.

There is the complaint that board members and others lack the *expertise* to interpret complex financial documents, which may hide unethical behavior. This is doubtless true in many cases. However, this only *makes* the case that we need ethics *in the professions*. Chief Financial Officer, Certified Public Accountants, Treasurers, Accounting Managers, and others all need to have good ethics.

Corporations will, of course, be best served with a culture that has good ethics woven throughout its practices. Organizations need to have ethics that go beyond the minimum that the law requires; they should not automatically accept their own or societal values when these seem questionable; they should not use the excuse that only young people can be ethically trained and formed; and ethics should be demanded of all the professions in the corporation.

⟋⟋⟋ **Question(s) to consider**: Imagine that you are manager of a department in a corporation that typically does not consider ethics. You hire an outside contractor to do some work for you—however, you have some ethical concerns about his past record. It seems that there has been some discrimination in his hiring of employees in the past. How do you handle what you consider to be an ethical problem? Make a written agreement with the contractor? Approach your supervisor for advice? Hire an ethical consultant to help out? Or, just do nothing? ⟋

Now, corporate culture is set from the top, down. The board and the CEO must show leadership by their own examples, as well as in the policies they and the corporation set. Ideally, training seminars should be provided for *each* profession, since each profession has its own set of temptations. Given the recent ethical lapses mentioned above, it is probably true that long-run profitability is usually enhanced with good ethics. Good ethics is a very serious business, indeed.

⟋⟋⟋ Group Discussion Questions

- How can bad ethics harm a corporation, and how badly?
- Is ethical training important today? If so, how do you answer the four objections listed in this chapter? ⟋⟋⟋

Part 2

Virtue: What Type of Person Should I Be?

To walk safely through the maze of human life,
one needs the light of wisdom and the guidance of virtue.

Buddha

Introduction

*We do not act rightly because we have virtue or excellence, but
we rather have those because we have acted rightly.*

Aristotle

*All that is necessary for the triumph of evil is
that good men do nothing.*

Edmund Burke 1729–1797,
Irish orator, philosopher, & politician

In the first part of this book, you read an overall perspective on ethics. Now you find out what kind of
person you should be: what does it mean to be moral? Here
we'll cover the ethics of character or "virtue."

This part of the book is divided into two sections:
- Ethics in your personal life.
- Ethics in your work life.

Different issues pertain to these two areas. However, the
particular virtues required for personal life and work life
frequently overlap. In this section we will tackle issues such
as why be moral at all, the true meaning of love, how to be-

have towards others with whom you work, and what makes a meaningful work life.

14

Why Be Moral?

"It is curious—curious that physical courage should be so common in the world, and moral courage so rare"

Mark Twain

"I never did, or countenanced, in public life, a single act inconsistent with the strictest good faith; having never believed there was one code of morality for a public, and another for a private man"

Thomas Jefferson

Morality is not properly the doctrine of how we may make ourselves happy, but how we may make ourselves worthy of happiness.

Immanuel Kant

From a personal viewpoint, let's ask the questions: "Why be moral (virtuous) in the first place?" and

"Why are we talking about morality here?" Today, in the Information Age, virtue includes among other traits: cooperation, persistence, creativity, the ability to plan ahead, regard for the welfare of others, trust in the future, flexibility, acting based on knowledge, and patience—patience to wait for *long-term* results. These virtues quite simply make an employee valuable and contribute to success and meaning at work and in society. It's easy to see their practical merit and, therefore, why one should be ethical. These virtues also protect others from mistreatment; they protect human dignity.

> ✐✐✐ **Question(s) to consider**: Have you ever taken a good look at if you really are moral? Or is it something you haven't done or never really thought about? You know why you'd like to be in physical shape and think about it a lot (maybe too much). Do you give as much thought to morality: not just yourself, but about others when you read the paper?
> ✐

There is another reason to be moral. It's the old adage, "Virtue is its own reward." That is, virtue contributes to individual human happiness and flourishing. Take the classical virtues, for example. The vices (as opposed to virtues) make one miserable and are likely to be looked down at by others. The virtues of justice, courage, temperance (restraint, self-control), and prudence (cautiousness) are the direct opposites of the vices: injustice, cowardice, excessiveness, and recklessness. Do we know many people who are unjust and cheat, and are happy? Are cowards happy? Are those who are excessive and reckless happy? We know that they are not.

Therefore, let's begin a study of the personal virtues. First in one's work life, then in personal life.

✐✐✐ Group Discussion Questions

- Give two reasons to be a moral individual.
- What virtues do you think are required in the information age? ✐✐✐

15

Virtue in Your Personal Life: The Meaning of Love

One can live magnificently in this world, if one knows how to work and how to love, to work for the person one loves and to love one's work.

Tolstoy's advice to his almost-fiancée, Valery Arsenev

This insightful quote from Tolstoy reminds us of the importance of two things necessary "to live magnificently": work and love. Five O'Clock Clubbers already have the best method in the world for finding work that they do well and enjoy doing. So, let's tackle the question of love. In other sections of this book, we draw on insights from Buddhism and Islam, but for now we will tap the Christian tradition.

The briefest definition one might give for love in the Christian sense is this:

Love pertains to our social nature and means "to intend the good of the other."

Our Social Nature

These ideas are more radical than they may seem at first blush. Let's begin with the basic teachings about our social nature: From the beginning "male and female God created them" (Genesis 1:27). But this is just the beginning, since people naturally form other communities with their extended families, in their neighborhoods, at work, through professional associations, and via various other civic, religious, and political associations. So, by their innermost nature, people are social beings, and unless we relate ourselves to others we can neither live nor develop to our potential.

Intending the Good of the Other

Christianity teaches that we are *social by nature* and we are strongly urged to love one another. But just what does it mean to love another? The Scriptures provide examples of God's love for Her/His people.

Again and again in the Hebrew Scriptures, God is described as caring for people. God saves Israel from its enemies and through His loyal people feeds the hungry, shelters the homeless, and favors the outcasts, widows, and orphans.

For Christians, Jesus represents a dramatic continuation

of "intending the good of others." God so loved the world that He gave His only son, Jesus, to the world. Jesus fed the hungry, and befriended outcasts, criminals, the poor, and the homeless. Jesus sacrificed himself for the good of others—even though he knew in the end he would be betrayed by someone close to him.

So love concerns our social nature and means to intend the good of the other person. These are radical ideas today.

The conception of love as *To intend the good of the other* is quite a radical departure from the contemporary popular understanding of love.

Love Undermined Today

It turns out that, in the modern world, this concept of love actually faces an uphill battle. First of all, the idea that we are social by nature is no longer as commonly accepted as it once was. To cite but one trivial example, membership in bowling leagues is down, while participation in bowling is up. The unrelenting momentum of rugged individualism continues to erode our sense of community, our feelings of being oriented toward others. The (false) view is that each person can find fulfillment alone and narcissistically apart from others. This common view is *irreconcilable* with basic Christian ideas, and is a source of great loneliness and a failure to find fulfillment.

Second, the concept that love means to *intend the good of the other* is a radical departure from the contemporary popular understandings of love, some silly and even infantile. For example, there is the idea that love is a "feeling" (hence the high divorce rate because the feeling passes); that love is conditional, that it is based on what one gets in return; or there is the absurdity that love equals good sex. These misunderstandings, of course, result in misery instead of fulfillment.

Even the concept that we are social by nature can no longer be taken for granted. For example, bowling is up while participation in bowling leagues is down!

Christians who adhere to authentic understandings of love are radical in today's culture. The cultural momentum, which sees everything, including *people,* as a means to one's own happiness, has become almost overwhelming. One marries, has children, and participates in groups, aiming only to find happiness for oneself instead of *intending the good of the other.*

This is nothing new, of course. Aristotle recognized the misunderstanding of love and friendship so common today. He spoke of relationships based on *utility* (the other person is somehow useful to us) and relationships based on *pleasure* (the other person is simply pleasurable to be with for whatever reason). These are inherently fragile relationships.

People who take seriously the idea that love is to intend the good of the other are actually a prize in today's culture.

> *✎✎✎* **Question(s) to consider**: Are most of your relation-
> ships based on utility (people who are useful to you)? Arte
> they primarily based on pleasure (choosing people who are
> good looking, rich or whatever)? Or are they primarily based
> on virtue (choosing to be around people of virtue)? *✎*

**Aristotle spoke of fragile relationships based on utility
(the other is somehow useful to us) or on pleasure
(the other is pleasurable to be with).**

Saint Valentine Intended the Good of the Other

The story of St. Valentine, a priest and martyr, is clouded by legend. According to one tradition, he defied the order of Emperor Claudius II banning engagement and marriage in Rome. Claudius II had difficulty in recruiting men for his armies. He reasoned that he might replenish the military if men had no attachments or young families. Valentine, believing the decree was unjust—and intending the good of others—continued to perform marriages in secret for young lovers, and was put to death when the emperor found out. He suffered martyrdom on February 14th around the year 270.

Although we're not matchmakers, it is part of the Five O'Clock Club's corporate mission *to intend the good of others*.

Thus, St. Valentine is a good role model for self-sacrificial love. He is also a champion for romantic love, no matter how much the modern Valentine's Day holiday has been sentimentalized and debased by superficial understandings of love.

If Tolstoy is correct about the need for love, then romantic love may well be a part of your Forty-Year Vision®. The basic data of the Christian tradition presented here may be helpful to you as you pursue your own romantic goals. Although we're not matchmakers, it is part of our corporate mission to *intend the good of others,* and our Valentine to you is actually printed on the inside front cover of every issue of our magazine:

The Garden of life is abundant, prosperous and magical. In this garden, there is enough for everyone. Share the fruit and the knowledge. Our brothers and we are in this lush, exciting place together. Let's show others the way. Kindness. Generosity. Hard work. God's care.

Love Explored—the Rest of the Story

Love pertains to our social nature and means to intend the good of others. This contrasts genuine love to false contemporary misconceptions.

Relationships based on either utility or pleasure are not loving in the deepest sense. These are inherently fragile relationships, since the time can come when the other person is no longer useful to us, or serves as a source of pleasure.

What does it mean *in practice* to intend the good of another person? How does this apply in our everyday work and personal lives?

First, we must have a working understanding of the human being. Here is the understanding that we have presented before. Feel free to modify and improve it. No final definition is possible, but, again, consider the six characteristics of a human being, this time in regard to love.

**Six traits that characterize a person:
material, spiritual, social, fragile, creative and free,
and equal in basic dignity.**

Love can be practiced in what we ordinarily might consider surprising ways. *Love toward our fellow man* generally can be practiced everywhere, including the workplace.

Intending the good of the other means to assist and support others as beings who are material, spiritual, social, fragile, free and creative, and equal in basic dignity. (See Table 1.)

🖉🖉🖉 **Question(s) to consider**: As you read through Tables 1 and 2, you could put checkmarks next to those entries that you feel are important to you and that you practice. For the unchecked items, is there something simple you could do so you could check them off at some time? 🖉

Doing good to others is not a duty, it is a joy,
for it increases our own health and happiness.

Zoroaster

Table 1: How to Love (i.e., intend the good of) Your Neighbor at the Workplace

Characteristics of Human Beings	Definition	Application
1. Material	A person requires food, clothing, shelter, etc., to survive.	Payment of just wages and benefits. Safe and pleasant working conditions.
2. Spiritual	A person must have "space" to practice spirituality.	Respect and encouragement for various belief systems. Time or days off for religious holidays are very important.
3. Social	A person only develops to his/her fullest with others.	Employees should have opportunities to socialize, work, and participate in cooperative settings, and join appropriate associations.
4. Fragile	We are all prone to error, have our weaknesses and failings.	Employees need oversight, second chances, extra training, or re-assignment.
5. Free and Creative	We all want to move forward professionally, to exercise our creative abilities.	Assignments should be made so responsibility falls to the lowest level possible.

Then There's Romantic Love

What does it mean to intend the good of another person in *romantic* love on a daily basis? Table 2 gives you an idea of how to do that. The same categories apply, that is, assisting and supporting a person who is material, spiritual, social, fragile, free and creative, and equal in basic dignity.

Of course, the list is illustrative and not exhaustive of what it means to intend the good of the other in romantic love. You might have fun adding ideas, based on the relationship with *your* spouse. There may even be a way to transfer *some* of the ideas from this table to your workplace.

Table 2: How to Love (i.e., intend the good of) Your Significant Other

Characteristics of Human Beings	Application
1. Material	Partners work, earn income, cook, clean for one another.
2. Spiritual	Partners practice their belief system together if possible, thereby exponentially increasing spiritual growth. Almost any spiritual teacher will verify the benefits of joint prayer.
3. Social	Marriage requires maintenance in its social context. Love is not only a feeling but also a commitment and hard work that other people can also celebrate and affirm.
4. Fragile	Marriage is NOT really a contract; it is a covenant. That is, forgiveness, assistance, and long suffering are ALL included. You know your partner's vulnerable spots and should not exploit them. Human fragility is perhaps a most overlooked factor.
5. Free and Creative	The parties intend each other's good in all respects in terms of his/her creative potential. When your partner succeeds, the proper response is celebration and joy, not jealousy.
6. Equal	Partners work, cook, clean for one another in an equitable arrangement of duties. While constant measuring should be avoided, neither gender should be systematically disadvantaged by the assignment of duties. Equality means that no one should be belittled.

✐✐✐ Group Discussion Questions

- What is the popular meaning of love?
- What is a better idea about what love is?
- Discuss the table, "How to Love Your Neighbor at the Workplace," and evaluate. ✐✐✐

16

Raising Children Well
(Not as Complex as It Seems)

*One should guard against preaching to young people success
in the customary form as the main aim in life. The most
important motive for work in school and in life is pleasure
in work, pleasure in its result, and the knowledge of
the value of the result to the community.*

Albert Einstein

The number of studies about what children need is
large and the conclusions often differ. As mothers increasingly entered the workforce, for years we heard about the
socializing *benefits* of day care and preschool. Then, *The New
York Times* reported (April 18, 2001) that children who spend
more than 30 hours a week in child care "are more demanding, more noncompliant, and they are more aggressive."

For years, experts had emphasized the benefits of academic formation at an early age. But now experts emphasize

the importance of "emotional intelligence," interpersonal skills, and developing a child's spirit, as opposed to academic intelligence in which parents teach with flash cards, learning toys, and so on. Of course, the "experts" can overturn all of this with the next study.

Parents pay for food, toys, activities and other things that the latest studies promise will be good for our children. But there is a lurking suspicion that everything cannot rest on the "latest study," and that the choices are not as "either/or" as they are often represented. After all, parents have been raising baby humans for tens of thousands of years, and we are not doing all that well now—even with all of our scientific studies!

It might help to step back a bit and remind ourselves that children need a variety of things *in common-sense measure*. Our way of understanding people, again, is to see them as material, spiritual, social, fragile, free and creative, and equal beings. Children have needs that correspond to *all* six of these aspects. The table in this chapter provides examples of what it might mean to meet these needs for children.

Children need love, especially when they do not deserve it.

Harold Hulbert

Of course, good parents do not need to consult a table every day to show them how to raise their children. Nevertheless, it can help parents to keep these basics in mind. The impact, when one or more of these is lacking, can be devastating for childhood and later life. To want for basic necessities, spiritual guidance, friendship, forgiveness, mental challenge, or self-esteem will almost certainly damage body and character. Living as we do in a culture that so highly values material goods, competition, freedom, and equality, perhaps the prudent thing to do is to emphasize the aspects that receive less attention: *spiritual life, cooperative relationships, and human frailty.*

Parents with good sense, who care about the comprehensive good of the child, and who show *practically* and *daily* that they care, are the real foundation for a childhood that blossoms into a well-adjusted adult life.

> *✐✐✐* **Question(s) to consider**: How much time do you spend with your children? How much attention do you pay to who their friends are, what they eat, how they're doing in school, and what they *value*? *✐*

How to Love (i.e., intend the good of) Your Children

Characteristics of Children	Sample Application
1. Material	A child requires food, clothing, shelter, etc. You may know how they should eat, but fail in the follow-through.
2. Spiritual	A child must have guidance in a spiritual tradition. Otherwise progress in this aspect will be retarded.
3. Social	A child only develops to his/her fullest with others. Children should have opportunities to socialize, participate, work in cooperative settings, and join appropriate clubs.
4. Fragile	Children make mistakes; they need oversight, and second, third, fourth (etc.) chances, as well as extra training.
5. Free and Creative	We can help children to grow intellectually to express their various talents. Knowledge of phonics, reading, shapes, colors, arithmetic, are important building blocks.
6. Equal	Children have a basic equality regardless of race, color, creed, etc. Society should see to equal opportunity.

We have **boldfaced** the aspects under-emphasized in American culture and that parents would do well to emphasize.

*The quickest way for a parent to get a child's attention
is to sit down and look comfortable.*

Lane Olinhouse

✐✐✐ Group Discussion Questions

- Does the author consider raising children overly complex?
- Discuss the table in this chapter and evaluate. ✐✐✐

17

Raising Children with Prudence

Discipline your son in his early years while there is still hope.
If you don't you will ruin his life.

Anonymous

*I*t is amazing how much about one's childhood can be revealed during an in-depth career counseling session. A person's basic ideas and character are formed during childhood, and it is impossible to escape these. You can move *through and beyond* certain ideas and character traits, but *never around them.*

Childhood Experience: The Starting Block

Career coaches hear various complaints:
- I never learned discipline as a child, and find it difficult to discipline myself now to do what is necessary for my (job) search.

- I perform poorly, since I have always had low self-esteem.
- No amount of salary seems to satisfy me. I always need, or at least want, more money.
- I have problems with superiors, since I never learned respect for authority as a child.
- I have problems with my peers, since I never learned to be social. I was very selfish when I was young.

🍃🍃🍃 **Question(s) to consider**: Do any of these ring a bell with you? How loudly? 🍃

These complaints are rooted in a childhood without sufficient discipline, self-esteem, generosity, respect for authority, and sociability. The career coach must take such a childhood and its effects as givens (you cannot ignore them); however, the client can work on them and to some degree move past them.

Raising children is difficult, and, it seems, no good deed goes unpunished. Those of us who are parents must be parents for the joy of a relatively well-adjusted child. This is the main reward to raising children. The question remains: How does one raise a child to become a relatively well-adjusted adult?

Raising Children and Using Prudence

Discipline, self-esteem, generosity, respect for authority, and sociability are actually things one can have too little or too much of. In other words, parents raising children must strike a prudent balance, or a "mean between extremes" when raising children.

We can guide children with proper discipline, or we can either be too harsh and restrictive, or too lax and libertarian. Instead of teaching children proper generosity, we can teach them stinginess on one hand or profligacy on the other. The table below shows several virtues and their extremes—applied either too little or in excess—or in the proper amount. The daunting challenge for the parent is to help the child hit the proper mean as nearly as possible. This produces the overall happiest child and well-adjusted adult.

Of course, the table shows only several virtues. A list like this could be constructed for many, if not all, of the virtues. It seems that the vices of Column III occur more frequently these days than the vices of Column I. While we hope that the center column is most common, it seems that libertarian, stingy, defiant, and self-centered young people may be in greater numbers than overly restricted, tepid, and excessively generous ones who have negative self-images. In any case, virtues help to make a well-adjusted adult in and out of work. Parents must accept the responsibility for guiding their children properly. If they do not, the consequences are likely to be considerable career (and other) counseling in later life.

I.	II.	III.
When In Excess	**Virtue**	**When Lacking**
Harsh or too restrictive	Discipline	Libertarian
Profligacy	Generosity	Stingy
Tepid and fearful	Respect for authority	Defiant
Negative self-image	Self-esteem	Self-centered

✐✐✐ Group Discussion Questions

• Is it true that you can move through and beyond certain ideas and character traits, but never around them? How so?

• Study the table in this chapter and evaluate if the details are TRUE or not. ✐✐✐

18

On Gratitude

If you pick up a starving dog and make him prosperous,
he will not bite you. This is the principal difference
between a dog and a man.

Mark Twain

We should all learn gratitude if we want to be genuinely happy. Gratitude is most certainly a virtue; and a virtue is a positive habit of character that helps one to act in a reasonable and constructive way. The full exercise of this virtue involves three steps:

1. One first recognizes the need for gratitude as a response to a favor;

2. One then should express gratitude in word; and,

3. One should express gratitude in deed.

In this way, gratitude comes to full fruition and brings no small amount of pleasure to all parties concerned.

🖉🖉🖉 **Question(s) to consider**: On Mark Twain's scale, which end are you closest to? A dog or a man? 🖉

Recognition of the Need for Gratitude

Humility is a virtue integral to gratitude. We cannot recognize the need for gratitude without it. People who are puffed up with their own accomplishments and who do not see how dependent they are on others and economic systems that have favored them are rarely grateful. They are blind to the ways in which they have been favored, perhaps beyond what they deserve. Therefore, the vice of pride is the death of humility.

> 🖉🖉🖉 **Question(s) to consider**: Have you ever made a gratitude list? Some people say that doing this often helps them to maintain emotional and spiritual balance. Remember: Thanksgiving is only *one* day of the year. What about the other 364? 🖉

In his classic work, *The Theory of Moral Sentiments*, Adam Smith, the father of modern economics, argues that people (even as economic agents) who don't feel gratitude are cheating themselves out of happiness. "Failing to feel grateful to those who came before is such a corrosive notion, it must account at some level for part of our bad feelings about the present. The solution—a rebirth of thankfulness—is in our self-interest. . . . For us not to feel grateful is treacherous selfishness."

Gratitude in Word

Gratitude is also a form of courtesy, which is mindful of how others have been helpful, and reciprocates in word. We have all felt the annoyance or even outright pain when people fail to **verbalize** gratitude for something significant we have done for them. This is not only ingratitude, but also rudeness. Think about your friends or coworkers whom you have helped without receiving a word of gratitude for your good deeds. This is painful indeed. Also think about this: You can enhance the good reputation of those who do good deeds when you speak a kind word about them to others. Hence, expressions of gratitude bring further rewards.

Adam Smith, the father of modern economics, argued that those who don't feel gratitude are cheating themselves out of happiness.

Gratitude in Deed

Gratitude for things large and small should also be repaid by appropriate actions. There are many such occasions in the world of work. People who want to benefit from having a "team of advisors"—a recommended technique for getting advice from those who are more senior than you who help you to move along in your career—should be careful to express gratitude with deeds. Do you simply take from people?

If you do not give back and show gratitude, even by helping those less fortunate than you, you risk proving Mark Twain right in his analysis of the difference between a dog and a man.

Gratitude for Life in General

According to gratitude guru Gregg Easterbrook, author of, *The Progress Paradox: How Life Gets Better While People Feel Worse,* "Those who describe themselves as being thankful to others, or to God, or to 'Creation in general' have more vitality, suffer less stress and experience fewer episodes of clinical depression. Well, aren't they the lucky ones? Grateful people are less materialistic, less concerned with status, less controlling and arrogant .. . than the population at large."

Beyond gratitude for specific things, there is a second type of gratitude. Let's call it gratitude for life in general. For those who believe in God, Allah, or some Source of being itself, that deity, as the Source of life, is the object of this gratefulness. This is a personality trait characterized by happiness for gifts one has received. It is a positive attitude that can produce a buoyant personality. The attitude is not simply being grateful for some specific things, but for life in general.

This feeling of gratitude for being or reality in general can also mean being grateful for what one does not have. Since this belief assumes that that basic reality (or God) is essentially benevolent, it is assumed that there are good reasons for not having things, as well.

Thankful people have more vitality, less stress, and fewer episodes of depression.

Gratitude for being also requires humility, since it recognizes the gifts given by God Him/Herself. Pride—here meaning the opposite of humility— makes the recognition of the gifts impossible. The self-made person does not understand the gifts he has received, and therefore is blind to the need for gratitude. In this context, gratitude is also often expressed in a special word, which is called prayer.

Gratitude for being also plays itself out in good deeds. It brings a person to do good deeds to others because of the sense of gratitude to God. The good things from God are passed on to another.

✐✐✐ Group Discussion Questions

• What do humility and gratitude have to do with each other?

• What is gratitude for life in general? What benefits does it have for the individual? ✐✐✐

19

Violence

Two years after the Columbine tragedy, some believe the continuing spate of school shootings proves the nation has made little progress in preventing or understanding this particularly horrific type of violent behavior.

Friday, April 20, 2001, by Robin Wallace, FOX news

The country that carried out the greatest number of known executions of child offenders was the USA.

Amnesty International

*O*ur nation continues to grapple with the reality of children killing children, the tragedy of Columbine being one example. Two years later, a fifteen-year-old freshman at Santana High School in Santee, California, killed two classmates and injured thirteen others in a wild shooting incident.

Communities have sought to prevent such outbreaks in the future. Methods of doing so have included attempts to identify troubled youths who might potentially do such things and to counsel them. Increased security measures include having the police present on campus. The use of metal detectors at school entrances is more common. Of course, even the slightest threat of violence is taken more seriously than it was years ago. One may not speak of such violence at school any more than one may even joke or speak about a bomb at an airport.

These measures certainly have their place, given the situation at schools. However, in the context of our violent society, these appear as glorified Band-Aids to a much, much larger problem. And, although school violence is horrific and a great human tragedy, it is not surprising or incomprehensible in the context of American society. We have made these little children what they are.

To generalize, we are sometimes a violent and not very gentle people. Consider these things:

· The U.S. imprisons a larger percentage of its people than does any nation on planet Earth. It has been said that if you are not truly angry and violent when you enter, you will be by the time you are released.
· This country is in the minority of countries that still exercise a death penalty. Also, we are known all over the world for fantastically long sentences and high prison populations of children and adults:

- According to Amnesty International, six countries since 1990 are known to have executed prisoners who were under eighteen years old at the time of the crime—Iran, Nigeria, Pakistan, Saudi Arabia, the United States, and Yemen. The country that carried out the greatest number of known executions of child offenders was the United States. The execution of children is true barbarism. Children simply lack the mental capacities for assessment, deliberation, choice, and responsibility that adults have.
- According to Amnesty International, since 1973 more than 90 U.S. prisoners have been released from death row after evidence emerged of their innocence of the crimes for which they were sentenced to death.
- A number of states permit their residents to own and carry handguns. Indeed, at this writing, our President comes from Texas, which is such a state. The implicit message is: The ability to kill might be something a citizen needs to exercise in this society.
- Television and movies continue to glorify violent solutions to human problems. The lesson: violence is THE answer. Of course, children and adults watch television incessantly.
- A competitive understanding of human relations is common these days, resulting in everything from jealousy to road rage.

· Family economics being what they are, we must
often leave the raising of our young to third parties
and this can retard the process of their socialization.
The New York Times (April 18, 2001) reports, as
noted previously, that (according to Dr. Jay Belsky,
one of the study's principal investigators) children
who spend more than 30 hours a week in child care
"are more demanding, more noncompliant, and
they are more aggressive." He adds, "They scored
higher on things like 'gets in lots of fights, cruelty,
bullying, meanness, as well as talking too much, and
demands must be met immediately.'" The research
was financed by the National Institute on Child
Health and Human Development and is the largest
and longest term study of childcare in the United
States.

So, the problem of violence is really systemic to
our culture, and will have no serious solution until
it is addressed as a systemic problem on political,
economic, and moral cultural levels. Band-Aids
alone will not suffice.

♪ ♪ ♪ **Question(s) to consider**: What do you do that en-
courages your children (or others) to be violent or bully others? How do you contribute to social violence yourself such
as by supporting the death penalty when so many have been
found innocent, or sending children to prison with adults?

How do you deescalate potentially violent situations in your own life? 🖋

On the brighter side, it is entirely possible to begin comprehensive measures to address the violence in this society. Prison policies are a matter of choice and can be changed. The elimination of the death penalty, better treatment of children caught in the system, and more creative solutions and alternatives to long sentences seem indicated. The carrying of guns is a dangerous and hopelessly antiquated practice that has no place in the life of the ordinary citizen. Tax policies might make it possible for a father or mother to remain home to raise children at least in the very early years.

We certainly do not know all the answers at this point. However, the direction seems clear.

🖋🖋🖋 Group Discussion Questions

• How has the tragedy at Columbine changed the way we think? What does it mean to say the response is a glorified bandage?

• Consider the possible solutions at the end of this chapter. Can you add to them? Do you agree with the solutions?
🖋🖋🖋

20

Virtue in Your Work Life: What Makes a Meaningful Work Life?

If a man is called to be a street sweeper, he should sweep streets even as Michelangelo painted, or Beethoven played music, or Shakespeare wrote poetry. He should sweep streets so well that all the hosts of heaven and earth will pause to say, here lived a great street sweeper who did his job well.

Rev. Martin Luther King, Jr.

While virtues contribute to productivity, they are also necessary to possess so as to make work meaningful. Let's review the virtues and vices, as presented in Part I, with different eyes here (see the table below).

Cooperation, hard work, creativity, optimism, planning ahead, concern for the welfare of others, trust, flexibility, and patience characterize the new approach to work. These virtues also support having work that is meaningful. How can work be meaningful if there is ruthless competition, workaholism, disconnectedness, possessiveness, and more? Work simply can't be. People should not be required to check their positive values at the door when entering the workplace. Clearly, most of us do not find meaning under harsh and oppressive conditions.

Meaningful Professions

As Reverend Martin Luther King, Jr., said above, everyone can have (or create) a job that is meaningful and satisfying. Examples abound in the professions. Think of entrepreneurs who strike out to do things that are from their heart. Think of the successful businessperson who manages employees by seeing to their professional growth, assuring fair treatment, and, at the same time, striving to meet departmental goals. Think of the doctor who treats patients and sees them return to productive life; the lawyer who can help people to achieve justice (we hope); and the clergy who care for the soul and see to spiritual wholeness. It is not hard to see that the virtues in the table play a vital role in all professions to various degrees. These virtues make professional work meaningful.

However, aside from the professions, do meaningful jobs exist in today's labor market? Can *everyone* have meaningful work? How about truck drivers, waiters, and laborers—can their occupations be meaningful, just like those of professionals? Yes, with one proviso (condition) that will be discussed later on.

A Question of Perception

It is sometimes a matter of perception whether or not a job is meaningful. It seems obvious that entrepreneurs, doctors, and other professionals mentioned above can have meaningful work. They should (hopefully) be walking testimonials to the virtues that were brought to light. But meaningful work can exist outside of the professions.

Perception is often the key. Reverend King's street sweeper is a prime example of how a working person can find pride and achievement in his work. So is a waiter who looks at his/her job in a positive way, rather than simply seeing the work as something that lacks the kind of control over circumstances and effect on people that are true of, say, doctors. The waiter is, one might say, a minister of hospitality. He is one who serves food, which is, of course, necessary for life. Further, the waiter's attitude helps to determine the quality of the meal. This is no small thing. Meals are a special time for us: they are times for celebration, important family gatherings or reunions, business dealings, and just enjoying being with someone who means something to us. Nothing is small about this, even if we dine alone. Waiters certainly can show

regard for the welfare of others, and demonstrate cooperation, trust, patience, and other virtues, besides just getting
the order right.

Now, consider truck drivers. Their behavior on the road
is especially important to city dwellers, both to drivers and
pedestrians. Not only is there skill involved in driving a large
vehicle, but also there must be regard for the welfare of others, patience, and cooperation (with other drivers). We have
all seen truck drivers who allow people to navigate the road
safely, as well as pull over to help other drivers in emergen-
cies. If a trucker doesn't have these good qualities, the outcome could be road rage. People with road rage have even
killed others. Further, given the grueling hours many people
spend commuting, it's no small thing for truck drivers to show
regard for the welfare of other drivers, as well as patience,
and cooperation.

> *✎✎✎* **Question(s) to consider**: Do you feel that your
> work is meaningful? Do you do anything to help those
> you work with to have more meaning in their jobs? *✎*

The Proviso

Working-class people are vulnerable in a way that professionals are typically not. Usually, doctors, lawyers and the
like earn enough (or more than enough) to live comfortably,

while, truck drivers, laborers and waiters, among others, face insecurity in this matter. It is not only the intrinsic nature of the work that counts, but also the extrinsic reward.

Compensation must be enough such that the individual is able to be self-supporting. Most of us can support ourselves (food, housing, transportation, and others) through our wages. Few live off of interest income or an inheritance. It is for this reason that economic ethicists have so fervently insisted on a just wage. Such a wage is also an essential ingredient for meaningful work. Without it, there is gross injustice and really no chance that work will be meaningful.

Virtues and Vices for a Meaningful Work Life

Virtues: Consistent with the Vision	Vices: Inconsistent with the Vision
Cooperative	Excessively competitive
Hard-working, persistent	Entitlement mentality; workaholic
Creative and optimistic	Zero-sum mentality
Planning ahead	Indifferent and haphazard
Regard for the welfare of others	Out-of-context behavior
Trust in the future	Siege mentality
Flexible	Rigid, unable to cope with organic change
Activity based on knowledge	Disconnected activity
Sharing, generous, patient for long-term results	Closed and possessive; focused on short-term interests

> *Management is doing things right;*
> *leadership is doing the right things.*

Peter F. Drucker,
American Management Guru

🌿🌿🌿 Group Discussion Questions

- What is meant by having a meaningful work life?

- Give examples of a meaningful work life.

- Can everyone have a meaningful work life?

- What do you think of the Reverend King's quote at the start of the chapter? 🌿🌿🌿

21

One Economy "Under God"?

"Bringing spirituality into the workplace violates the old idea that faith and fortune don't mix. But a groundswell of believers is breaching the last taboo in corporate America."

Fortune Magazine, July 9, 2001

*W*e are all acquainted with The Pledge of Allegiance, which puts the nation under God, basically from a political view: *"I pledge allegiance to the flag of the United States of America and to the Republic for which it stands, one nation, under God, indivisible, with liberty and justice for all."*

Political power is used to govern the nation *under God*, with liberty, and with justice. However, what about God in other areas besides government? What about God and the workplace?

Putting the country under God in an economic sense is more challenging and controversial. *Fortune,* in the July 9,

2001 issue ("God and Business; The Surprising Quest for Spiritual Renewal in the American Workplace." pp. 58–80), chronicled a number of business leaders who were trying to do just that in their own businesses. They were convinced that their creative energy was somehow tied to the creative energy of God. They also believed that religion was not a purely and completely personal matter, since it impacts everyday life.

According to the article, putting business under God means a number of things from a practical perspective. The business leaders were starting various procedures that they thought were important, based on a spiritual understanding of business. Some of them were:

1. Do not let the pursuit of money and power replace God.

2. Realize that there is no higher calling than to serve God.

3. Slow down at work. Work from the soul.

4. Narrow the salary differentials from the least well-paid to the best paid.

5. Ethical behavior is rooted in character and, therefore, is important for who we are as businesspersons.

6. Err a bit on the generous side in company down-sizings.

7. Offer spiritual experimentation with retreats, prayer, meditation, and Eastern traditions.

8. Respect all living creatures, not just humans. Within reason, all animals deserve some protection.

9. Show accountability not only to stockholders, but also to employees, the community, and to other stakeholders.

10. Give new employees from disadvantaged backgrounds a try at responsibility.

A 1999 Gallup Poll reported that 78 percent of Americans said they felt a need to experience spiritual growth. *Since we spend most of our waking hours at work, we must look for this growth there, also.*

Pursuing meaning, which can include spiritual growth at work, is an individual thing, but the preceding list offers clues as to what it might look like. People are looking to find meaning by getting in touch with God, with themselves, and with others in ways that are kind, compassionate and constructive. Although the business leaders described in *Fortune* seem to be inspired by the ideas and practices of their religious denominations, they are certainly acting on their own. This is not only about moral rules, but it is also a quest to find meaning in what one does. It is an attempt to fill an emptiness in the daily work routine.

🖉🖉🖉 **Question(s) to consider**: What do you hold as your supreme value at work? How can you make your worklife more kind, compassionate and constructive? How can you make the same improvements in your personal life? Write down these things so you can implement them and check on yourself later. *🖉*

What is the alternative? The alternative is all around us. It's giving up the search for greater meaning, and living with a feeling of emptiness. Perhaps it's more usual to try to fill this emptiness by charging after power and money. Power and money are certainly false gods and those who chase after them neither thrive nor find true happiness. It also seems that some of these 10 practices must've had positive business results in terms of corporate reputation, employee morale, stockholder confidence, and compliance with the law.

🖉🖉🖉 Group Discussion Questions

• Are you surprised by the quote from *Fortune* magazine at the beginning of this chapter? What does it mean from your perspective? What is the alternative to this perspective?

• Discuss the ten points I picked out as important for a spiritual understanding of business. *🖉🖉🖉*

22

Avoiding Shipwreck:
Ethics and Entrepreneurship

*A business that makes nothing but money
is a poor kind of business.*

Henry Ford

So you want to be an entrepreneur? You will need the right stuff from a business standpoint: a new widget that's in demand; a great business plan; adequate capital; and a strategy to beat the competition, as well as the drive to do it. What's more, you've probably done what successful entrepreneurs do: You've picked a business you'll love.

But do you have the right *ethical* stuff—the right character to make your business successful? Will your business fail, as most startups do, because of character flaws?

Assume you won't break the law or cheat people. Beyond that, successful entrepreneurs possess—and continue to hone—special habits of character, that is, virtues. The four traditional linchpin virtues (usually thought of as the moderate path between the two extremes) go back at least as far as Aristotle. These classic human virtues have been already mentioned—prudence, justice, courage, and temperance. These four are characteristic of successful modern entrepreneurs. You can consciously make them part of *your* character—and avoid shipwreck for your business (see table below).

Linchpin Virtues

In excess:	Extravagance	Excessive caution	Self-negation	Cowardice
VIRTUE:	**JUSTICE**	**PRUDENCE**	**TEMPERANCE**	**COURAGE**
Inadequate:	Miserliness	Rash and impulsive	Self-indulgence	Foolhardines

Prudence

*If a wise man behaves prudently, how can he be overcome
by his enemies? Even a single man, by right action,
can overcome a host of foes.*

Saskya Pandita

A prudent (careful) person is someone who makes good decisions with long-term goals in mind. Prudence stands between the twin shipwrecks of excessive caution and thoughtless, impulsive action. The entrepreneur who is excessively cautious will never do what must be done: recognize new opportunities and methods. The real entrepreneur quite literally sees things (possibilities) that others cannot.

For example, by 1899, Henry Ford had produced a horseless carriage that was written up in the Detroit press. Shortly after, he had to choose between his steady job at Detroit Edison and his hobby, building the automobile. It was neither exercising excessive caution nor acting rashly when Ford made his choice. He recognized that his job at the electric company was a distraction from his life goals. In June 1903, Henry Ford and ten investors incorporated the Ford Motor Company.

Are you in the habit of doing research and analysis? Are you realistic and do you learn from your mistakes? Do you think and plan ahead? Are you impetuous? Do you act without thinking and judging? If you make sudden, unpredictable changes, are headstrong, and a daredevil, becoming an entrepreneur probably is not for you. The entrepreneur who is not cautious and careful will never navigate a straight course toward his or her goals; the likely outcome would be a violent shipwreck. It's much better first to get a job working for somebody else and then outgrow the daredevil mentality.

> 🖉🖉🖉 **Question(s) to consider**: When formulating your business plan, for example, did your financial projections take into account *prudence* in estimating your startup expenses for real estate, advertising and promotion? Too little budgeted might not attract enough business to get you into

the black; too much might leave you short in meeting some basic expenses (such as rent), especially if your projections for revenues are rash and unreasonably high. 🖋

Justice

> *When will our consciences grow so tender that we will act to prevent human misery rather than avenge it?*
>
> Eleanor Roosevelt

Justice is giving each party his or her due. It is a fatal flaw for an entrepreneur to be miserly or to fail to give people what they rightly deserve. Give employees credit when credit is due; fully use their talent; pay just wages; respect all stakeholders; and, especially, treat customers fairly.

If you are not just, you'll have angry employees, high turnover, potential penalties (or worse), and a bad reputation in the marketplace. Earnestly adopt a just frame of mind to guide even the smallest decisions. In the long run, it's impossible to hide even minor wrongs.

Courage

> *Without courage, wisdom bears no fruit.*
>
> Baltasar Gracian

Okay, you may have prudence and judgment, but can you also *act*? You've done the right research and made the proper analysis, but can you take reasonable risks and still sleep at night? Entrepreneurs need the courage to act and the courage to survive setbacks. As a capitalist (or founder of a nonprofit), you should feel bold when good opportunities and reasonable risks come your way; otherwise, at crucial moments, you'll fall victim to timidity or cowardice. It's appropriate to feel frightened when bad or unreasonable risks come along; otherwise, you may be just plain foolish. Indeed, you want to feel the right things, at the right time for the right reasons (think of Aristotle's use of "right").

> *✐ ✐ ✐* **Question(s) to consider**: Courage often requires support—going it alone can be tough. Do you have an adequate support system? Is your spouse on your side and is he/she willing to cut down on spending? Do you have peers you can turn to for business advice? The Five O'Clock Club urges its members to choose buddies with whom they can regularly speak to during their job-hunt period. Who is your buddy? Are in you in touch with your local chamber of commerce? The Small Business Association? *✐*

Temperance

Being forced to work, and forced to do your best, will breed in you temperance and self-control, diligence and strength of will, cheerfulness and content, and a hundred virtues which the idle will never know.

Charles Kingsley

Temperance—restraint and self-control—entails moderation, self-denial, discipline, and even austerity when necessary. Can you work industriously without reward for years (even Microsoft and McDonald's did not make a profit for over a decade)? Entrepreneurs put in long hours. Can you do that? If not, your ship is really a toy boat and it is better left floating safely in the bathtub.

You may think that being prudent, just, temperate, and courageous don't really add up to a business advantage. You may think that the real reward is simply *being* that way, and you would be correct. Still, it's better for you and for those around you if you do both: *Be* a good person in your everyday life and practice these virtues in your worklife, too. You will thrive personally as your organization thrives, and being moral also helps those around you to achieve excellence in the marketplace.

The virtuous entrepreneur promotes the common good through her or his own efforts. You too can be such a person. May your business navigate the rocky shoals ahead!

✐✐✐ Group Discussion Questions

• What does it mean concretely to "avoid shipwreck?" (think of the doctrine of the mean between extremes.)

• What are the linchpin virtues, and how do they apply to an entrepreneur?

• Can these virtues apply to you in the course of your personal and business life? ✐✐✐

23

Human Capital: The Key to Our Future

It is not so very important for a person to learn facts. For that he does not really need a college. He can learn them from books. The value of an education is a liberal arts college is not learning of many facts but the training of the mind to think something that cannot be learned from textbooks.

Albert Einstein

The speed and unpredictability of innovation create a need for considerable investment in human capital, according to Alan Greenspan, when he was Federal Reserve chief. Greenspan called for an educational system that integrates work and training, and that serves the needs of workers as *workers* throughout their life span. More dramatically, he said that businesses should not expect four-year colleges alone to create the pool of skilled workers that they will need. He called for business partnerships with community colleges

157

and public agencies to create the future worker. Then Labor Secretary Alexis Herman agreed. She said that we do not have a worker shortage in this country, but a *skills* shortage.

On these matters, Greenspan, Herman, and others speak quite correctly in two respects: the great importance of "human capital" for the new economy and the need to develop such persons as much as possible. But this is alarming, since the type of education our institutions provide has the economic man swallowing up the whole man.

Do we really want to weld together business and education, as some have suggested? Do we want the business community and its leaders to set the agenda for education? The answer is a resounding "NO." Today, the trend is to cut back on the traditional liberal core-course requirements, and emphasize courses that teach marketable skills. While the goals of a good education may include these practical courses, today, this is being done at the expense of providing a liberal education. Exactly what is the problem behind this?

The liberal arts college's core subjects are history, languages, literature, philosophy, and theology, among others—not professional or technical subjects. Without the liberal arts, the university creates highly skilled, but not truly civilized people. It does not contribute, as it should, to their personal development or to the common good.

Without a liberal education, students are deprived of the chance to consider questions concerning the importance and meaning of human life, of *their* lives. On their own, they will not give systematic consideration to such questions as: "What is man?"; "What is happiness?"; "What is the common good?"; "What is noble?"; and "What is not noble?" Such students neither read what great minds have said, nor consider the issues themselves. Further, the falling away from liberal education negatively impacts even the economic common good. Today's economy requires *persons* with a liberal background; that is, those who have a broad view of things, who are flexible, who see the connections between different areas of knowledge, and who understand their humanity and that of others.

> *♫♫♫* **Question(s) to consider**: The above paragraph poses five tough questions. Do you give these any thought? Answers to these are not simple. Pick the one that seems most important to you and, in a few sentences, write your answer. It *is* a tough job to come up with an answer and many have tried to answer them. So a little reflection may make you more aware of your place in the world. *♫*

The real problem is not a simple skills shortage. While many persons such as Greenspan, Herman, and others speak with good intentions about the economy and education, problematic assumptions lie buried in their thinking. (We should never assume that narrow specialists would have the proper vision of the whole.) Good intentions are not enough here; human life is about more than economics, and education, above all, must recognize this.

🪶🪶🪶 Group Discussion Questions

- What does "Human Capital" mean?
- Are good intentions enough?
- What is a liberal education, and why is it useful? 🪶🪶🪶

24

Five O'Clock Clubbers Talk about Their Good Habits

By David Madison, Ph.D., Director of The National Guild of
Career Coaches of The Five O'Clock Club

*The chains of habit are generally too small to be felt
until they are too strong to be broken.*

Samuel Johnson

ere, we present examples of the previously mentioned virtues that have helped some highly
successful Club members to get them where they are today.
These persons also talk about their resolutions for the future: What do they plan to do to keep up the good work in
the years ahead? Their stories illustrate how by having the
right virtues—and applying them to their business lives—the
results are often spectacular. Virtue proves not only to be its
own reward, but also is rewarded handsomely in the corporate world.

✎ ✎ ✎ **Question(s) to consider**: In reading through this chapter, there are great lessons to be learned. In these or similar situations, would you have done the same things—do you have the same character traits? If so, how can you or do you apply them in your career? Also, are there any character traits you need to overcome? *✎*

Sergio—From Factory Worker to CFO

A CPA with 25 years' experience in corporate America, Sergio owns a consulting business in Manhattan.

"When I was young, I was doing factory work, working with my hands. My efforts were always appreciated, but if I wanted to get ahead, I knew I was going to have to work with my head instead of my hands. And I've always had an ability to solve problems." It appears that finding a better way to do things became a driving principle in Sergio's life at an early age. Hence, he says that persistence and determination have played major roles in his life, or, as he puts it, "Chasing things to a conclusion, working hard to find an answer."

**Character traits: persistence and determination.
"Chasing things to conclusion." –Sergio**

While the CFO at an entertainment company, for example, he took on the challenge of turning around a manufacturing operation that supported international sales. Because of on-going production and supply problems, the president was on the verge of firing top executives. "If you want it fixed, give it to me," Sergio said. Refusing to accept disaster as a foregone conclusion, he took aggressive measures to find a solution. As CFO, he admits, "I would get to stop reporting that we were having problems in that area." He contracted for much larger office space, ordered the necessary equipment, established inventory control and a reliable order-entry system. Eventually, the department became a profit center. "There was no option. This was going to get fixed, and I was going to fix it."

"If you want it fixed, give it to me."–Sergio

But Sergio admits that good habits are sometimes hard to acquire. He still struggles with getting things done on deadline and managing people's expectations—and he identifies procrastination as the most difficult bad habit to break. But we can suspect that he probably sets high standards for himself, and doesn't come in behind schedule too often. "The end product," he says, "always comes from the same level of hard work."

This factory worker who became a CFO is the first to admit, however, that his own hard work isn't the only key to his success. A primary character trait with Sergio—right up there with persistence and determination—is trusting input from someone else. Above all, he credits his success to the "love, support and unswerving loyalty of my wife. She helps me in more ways than I could describe. But it's always been her belief in me that has allowed me to make the right and often, difficult, choices in my career."

Sergio is a graduate of The Five O'Clock Club program, and our methodology is reflected in the resolution that he has adopted: "Never stop a job search. Opportunities find you only if you seek them out. The consulting business that I'm in helps me to keep doing that. To be successful, we always have to promote ourselves, and I'm never going to stop doing that again."

Cecile—In the Internet since the Mid-1990s

Cecile is a Corporate E-Commerce Manager at a Fortune 100 company. "I realized early on in life that if I wanted to have mobility in my career and in my life, it would take a certain amount of dedication." For Cecile, the key to remaining dedicated to her goals has been high energy and focus. When she discovered the Internet in the mid-90s, she was able to give her career a boost by bringing her high energy and focus to use of the Internet. She recalls her early reaction, "This medium is so powerful. If someone can harness it for commerce and business, it's going to be incredible."

Character traits: high energy and focus. "I work on keeping a balance between self-confidence and humility." –Cecile

Harnessing her own hard-driving nature, in fact, is one of the areas in which Cecile is seeking self-improvement. She says that impatience is a bad habit she's trying to break. "I move fast, and I tend to be impatient with those who are not moving like I do, who are not as decisive. I'm even impatient with people in situations where those things aren't possible." She also recalls the words of a mentor, "The best business people have a balance between self-confidence—they know what they're capable of—and humility. They're not overly prideful. That delicate balance is always something I'm working on, where you have self-confidence and belief in yourself—and you can inspire that in others—but also the humility to tolerate shortcomings and faults."

"I maintain focus." –Cecile

As a Five O'Clock Club graduate, Cecile is no stranger to planning and goal setting, but resolutions tied to a particular date don't seem to play a big role in her plotting the future. "New Year's isn't necessarily the only occasion that triggers that." She hopes to keep "shaking things up" regardless of the time of year. "But then again, I'm working for a big company which wants to have things shaken up!" For the long haul, Cecile believes in simply maintaining her focus on the things that matter to her. She will continue to work toward building situations in which there is the right combination of creativity and leadership.

Blanche—Staying in Touch

Blanche is the Director of Manufacturing for accessories, dresses, intimate apparel, and children's wear for a major retailer.

Blanche attributes her success to a habit that she spent many years pursuing and perfecting: networking. She realized early on in her career, working as a buyer, that it makes good business sense to stay in touch with people, but the process was not really a burden because she came across so many people that she liked and genuinely wanted to stay in touch with. Although today she carries a PDA in her handbag, over the years she has relied mainly on the low-tech "little black book." Originally, it was a list of friends and family. When she began traveling to New York on business, she added restaurants and the "people I wanted to make a point of staying in touch with." And she prefers the phone to e-mail for keeping in touch with everyone.

Character traits: maintaining relationships. "I also keep a prioritized to-do list." –Blanche

Blanche's present position is proof of the value of maintaining connections. A store manager who once reported to her had previously worked at her current employer, and was able to put her in touch with key people who were instrumental in bringing her on board.

Blanche acknowledges that there is a good habit that she is working to acquire: "My goal is to touch a piece of paper only once!" She admits that "sorting is really the first touch," so maybe touching it twice is the best that can be hoped for. "I find I do a lot of shuffling, and I get very irritated with myself when I do that. After sorting, you shouldn't shuffle and reshuffle; do something with it."

She is also a firm believer in the to-do list, on which chores are categorized as Urgent, Before the End of the Day, or By the End of the Week. And she's trying to break the habit of being "too spontaneous," being lured into pleasant tasks that deflect her from the urgent ones. But the to-do list "works like a dream" especially in helping to maintain her focus on priorities. "When I don't do a to-do list, I still tend to get things done, but I tend to forget some things."

Mindful of The Five O'Clock Club advice that networking is a life-long pursuit, Blanche's resolution is no surprise: "To stay in better touch with the people I know and care about."

🍃🍃🍃 **Question(s) to consider**: Do you have a to-do list? Many of us do, but it's often too long and daunting. Do you break up your list the way Blanche does? 🍃

Gail—Have Something to Contribute

Gail is a public relations and marketing executive in Chicago. "I was an only child, and was told I could accomplish anything I wanted to." So, an upbringing with a positive slant played a role in shaping Gail's outlook and approach. But the positive outlook has been complimented with a few habits that are the foundation for her success. "I have always looked not only at the big picture, but also at the details. And I have learned to listen long and listen well"— a habit, she confesses, that was one of the most difficult to acquire. "We all know people who just can't wait until you've finished talking to put in their two cents' worth. Have they heard you? I don't think so." Developing her skills as a listener has helped Gail to maintain another good habit, namely, being kind to people. "Being kind has helped me a great deal. Having people at all levels on your side is wonderful." And having just turned fifty, she says that high energy is a crucial factor for success as the years add up. "No matter how old you are, you doggone well better have energy."

Character trait: listen long and listen well. "I focus on being kind to people." –Gail

Gail knows that these factors played a role in helping her land her current position. Her years of experience were crucial in being hired as national head of sales and marketing for a network of twenty-eight offices. But she had to listen well during interviews over the course of more than ten meetings—and she had to demonstrate that a woman "of her age" had the energy that the position demands.

Given the scope of her task, the avalanche of priorities that she faces daily, and her love of challenge, Gail says that the most difficult bad habit to break has been taking on too much. "I have learned to say, 'No, not right now.' I have found that it's fair to ask someone what his or her true deadline is, and then indicate whether or not it can be met."

"High energy is necessary today." –Gail

An enthusiastic graduate of The Five O'Clock Club in Chicago, Gail suggests making a resolution that calls to mind the purpose of our Seven Stories Exercise: "Continually assure yourself that you're good, that you have something to contribute. In other words, don't second-guess yourself. Have confidence in yourself. Believe in yourself."

> 🖋🖋🖋 **Question(s) to consider**: Gail has learned not take on too much. That's like Blanche's prioritizing her to-do list. How do you stand in dealing with too much, and feeling overwhelmed? 🖋

Timothy—The Eternal Optimist

Timothy is an advertising representative for the website of a major Maryland newspaper, handling major accounts in the arts and entertainment.

"I'm an eternal optimist," Timothy admits, and he sees two of his most important character traits, confidence and persistence, flowing from that. He credits the optimism to his upbringing, and confidence was gained through years working in broadcasting. "Radio demands that you be confident. Especially when you're on the air or making a presentation, the spotlight is on you. I know I'm capable of not only doing my work, but also doing it creatively and successfully."

Character traits: confidence and persistence.
"I combine these with planning and follow-through."
–Timothy

But being persistent, Timothy acknowledges, requires ongoing effort. He says that he is continually trying to improve on planning and follow-through. "I'm not by nature an organized person, it requires a lot of effort on my part. I've learned to create ways for me to be organized and to follow through on plans."

And The Five O'Clock Club gave him a boost in this respect as he was interviewing for his current position. "You need someone to remind you to stick to a plan. There are plans that work and require discipline." He ranks getting his job as a major success story that can be chalked up to persistence. He was accustomed to sending thank-you letters after interviews, but he took The Club's methodology to heart after interviewing with his current employer. He wrote a letter proposing what he could do to improve business, based on what went on during his interview. He was very interested, and he sensed that the feeling was mutual; smart follow-up, The Club advises, can make the difference. It certainly did in Timothy's case.

He submitted a proposal including content ideas for advertising. "They were impressed. If you like what you see, you have to work at it. They're not going to do all the work to hire you. Those cases are rare. If you want it, you have to show them that you do." By inclination, Timothy is alert to ways to help him improve on follow-through, and he found that The Club was a great match: "I got a lot out of what The Five O'Clock Club has to offer."

As an eternal optimist, Timothy is aware of the need for balance in life. Hence, he always hopes to do better at daily planning and follow-through, but also "to savor the small moments in life and read more books, with no missed opportunities."

Leon—Setting High Standards for Himself

Leon is a business development manager for a financial website in Philadelphia.

"The apple doesn't fall very far from the tree," Leon explains in tracing his good habits. He recalled that his mother opened her own business, a small gift shop, to fund some of the extras for her kids, such as summer camp.

So, he grew up with the idea that extra effort could make a difference in life, and decided to set high standards for himself. He recalls that he was unable to get into the very top business schools, but was accepted at Fordham, still, one of the better ones. "I perceived this as a setback. But I sought out the toughest courses and the toughest professors. I wanted to create the model of the top business school. Getting fluff grades might make some people feel good, but I knew that, in the real world, it's what you know, not inflated grades, that matters."

Character traits: hard work, high standards and going the extra effort. "The higher you climb, the better you need to be at managing your time." –Leon

In addition to the willingness to work hard, Leon traces his success to "my natural curiosity," love of learning, and research. His interest in research was satisfied by a prior career in journalism, and his move into an Internet company was based on doing extensive research. But he also acknowledges his people skills. "I'm a people-person. I've always been able to interview well, whether in a formal interview or a cocktail hour discussion."

The area of life in which Leon is seeking improvement, trying to banish his bad habits, is daily organization and time management. "The higher you climb the corporate ladder, the better you need to manage your time. It's a battle. Because we're a small company, I've had good exposure to the CFO and CEO. I watch these guys and I'm not afraid to ask, 'How do you manage all these projects?'" He's trying to strike the balance between attention to detail and keeping the big picture in mind. One valuable lesson he picked up from a time management course is: "If you look at something that's only going to take five minutes or less, address it right now. That way it'll be off your desk. Getting rid of a lot of little things can help jump start your day."

> *✐✐✐* **Question(s) to consider**: One common thread running through all of these stories is time management and dealing with all the "stuff." What's your approach to these issues? *✐*

Leon has come up with resolutions that involve more hard work and extra effort. He hopes to have his own business someday, and even now he is devoting time and energy to an enterprise that can be run on weekends. As he plots his future, Leon is keeping The Five O'Clock Club methodology in mind. "Make the plan. My life is a matter of connecting the dots. Today you always have to ask, 'How am I positioned to take the next step?'"

✐✐✐ Group Discussion Questions

• Give examples of how "Character traits: hard work, high standards and going the extra effort" promote a person's career.

• What other traits are needed for a good work life?

✐✐✐

25

Maintaining Focus
Having a Vision and Sticking to It: Those Who Get Ahead Find a Way to Focus

By Kate Wendleton, President of The Five O'Clock Club

Vision without action is a dream.
Action without vision is simply passing the time.
Action with Vision is making a positive difference.

Joel Barker

40-year-old client of mine was excited about his career plan, which we had just developed together. He thought that the direction was right and that it was comfortably attainable.

Yet as he was leaving my office he said, "But I'm afraid I may be offered work that would take me in a completely different direction. I may not be able to resist the challenge."

I told him he could "take the challenge" and give up his long-term vision. He would find himself headed in a different direction than the one he wanted.

> 🖉🖉🖉 **Question(s) to consider**: What does your equation: Vision + Action add up to? If one of these two variables changes, can you still make them add up? 🖉

Competent people get many "once-in-a-lifetime opportunities" that are impossible to refuse. As Garrison Keiller notes, "Once-in-a-lifetime opportunities come along all the time—just about every week or so."

As a career coach, I would advise you to develop your long-term plan. It's okay if the details are murky. You still need even a blurry vision to help you keep on track. You can develop a Forty-Year Vision to be thorough, but the fifteen-year mark is often the most important. (These exercises are in the Appendix of this book.)

When opportunities come your way, the decision is easier: If something fits in with your Fifteen- or Forty-Year Vision®, do it. If it doesn't, don't do it.

In the early days of running The Five O'Clock Club, I posted a one-page sheet of my vision beside my computer. I forced myself to look at it every day so I wouldn't forget where I was headed. It seemed as though every week someone had an idea for me—good ideas, perhaps, but they were "off strategy."

There were still other threats to my determined focus. At one point, I was consulting part-time for a major corporation while running The Five O'Clock Club the other eight days a week. My boss asked me if I would like to be the next head of the department. It took me over a month to turn the offer down. Even *I* could be taken off-course.

Life has a way of sneaking up and distracting us. People are happy when they are working toward their goals. When they get diverted from their goals, they are unhappy. When they don't know what their goals are, they often feel lost.

So take the time to develop your Fifteen- or Forty-Year Vision, perhaps by working with a Five O'Clock Club coach. Stay focused while remaining flexible in the market.

Part 3

Guidelines: What Must We Do?

(Ethical Principles for Action)

It is easy to perform a good action, but not easy to acquire a settled habit of performing such actions.

Aristotle

Introduction

But the most important lesson I have learned in my twenty years of research on morality is that nearly all people are morally motivated. Selfishness is a powerful force, particularly in the decisions of individuals, but whenever groups of people come together to make a sustained effort to change the world, you can bet that they are pursuing a vision of virtue, justice, or sacredness.

Johnathan Haidt,
Happiness Hypothesis: Finding Modern Truth in Ancient Wisdom
Why the Meaningful Life Is Closer Than You Think

In Part I, we looked at the basic perspective on ethics, and in Part II, issues of character where you decided the kind of person you wanted to be. It's now time to ask the question, "What must I *do* in various situations?" This section was saved for last since the way we act is determined by our perspective and the type of person we choose to be. A person of kindness, duty, courtesy, nobility, generosity, justice, prudence, courage, and temperance would answer questions of ethical import in a different way from those who don't possess these virtues.

So, here we shall answer the following questions:
- What does it mean to have "freedom?"
- How can I target appropriate goals?
- How can I stay on track in my actions?
- How can I terminate employees with dignity, as well as other topics related to the workplace.

As you may have guessed by this point, the core framework/perspective to answer these questions is the *preservation and promotion of human dignity*. Now that you better understand this framework, you may choose to adopt this perspective—or not. There are lots of alternatives, such as "greed is good!" How you choose to act is up to you.

26

Freedom, License, and a Way Out

The 19th century was about economic freedom. The 20th century was about political freedom. This century will be about Americans deciding for themselves what's moral and what's not.

Alan Wolfe in *The New York Times Magazine*,
March 18, 2001

Many today would agree in describing this age as one increasingly of freedom from moral codes; be they philosophical, social, and religious or other types. For Americans, often, character doesn't matter, virtue doesn't matter, and moral codes don't seem to matter. Bill Clinton absolutely demolished George H. W. Bush about twenty years ago when Bush tried to make character into a campaign issue. Americans tend rather to be interested in pragmatics and their pocket books.

Isn't freedom always a good thing, however applied?
No—just as the nineteenth century resulted in serious abuses
of the working man, including the horror of human slavery;
the twentieth century brought about the disaster of an elected
Führer in Germany, Communist oppression and mass murder
of civilians, and voter polarization and alienation in America;
so this new century of moral freedom may produce abuses
equivalent to slavery, Auschwitz, and the like. Quite a sober-
ing thought, but how can this happen (again!), you ask?

Freedom without restrictions can have drastic consequences.

There are many danger points in this young century, but
the largest danger lies in the area of medicine. The scientific
developments here are most astonishing, and we have even
mapped the entire human genome. This can give us unprecedented *power and control* over human life. Moral freedom
from all constraints other than law makes it likely that
some truly offensive experiments and *practices* will develop.
Without moral rules, or a shared understanding of the moral
order, why not eventually clone people? Why not have acres
full of warehouses stocked with cloned people who are used
for spare parts? Now *there's* a new and innovative form of
slavery. It will eventually be possible for any couple (or individual) to *breed* children for the exact characteristics they

desire. That power and control over nature will surely impact society, evolution, the ratio of males to females, and such.

Moral discussion can take place on at least five important levels as shown in the table below. Is there a shared moral code in effect on any of these levels that will stop these potential nightmares? Likely there isn't. In our society, is there at least enough moral dialogue that might bring about a shared moral understanding about character (virtues), about moral principles, or about moral rules? Clearly not. Individuals exercise their freedom increasingly without considering the guardians of our society's ethics: the churches, certain civic organizations, and scientific institutions. So what are we to do to develop a common moral grasp and thereby prevent disasters in this "century of moral freedom?"

Only a creative reconsideration of our religious, civic, and philosophical traditions can offer us hope. We must re-energize of all those carriers of moral tradition, those that form our character, that give us principles to live by, and that set rules and boundaries. These carriers include the nuclear family, the extended family, neighborhood associations, churches, the Boy and Girl Scouts, the P.T.A., and so on. Who can doubt that the ties that bind these groups together are weakening? Their re-energizing is our largest hope. This re-energizing might occur around the concept of human dignity.

We do have reason for hope. Perhaps there will be a reintegration of religious institutions into the pluralistic diversity of American life. There also seems to be a renewed understanding of the need for families and the community in raising a child to *responsible* adulthood. It "takes a whole village to raise a child" some say. Let's hope that such understandings are matched with appropriate action.

🖋🖋🖋 **Question(s) to consider**: In viewing this table, you would likely immediately think about yourself. But what about when you react with others? What are they like? How would you protect yourself if you needed to? 🖋

Level	Description
Meta–ethical	Why even be moral?
The person	What type of character (virtues) should be aspired to?
Principles	What general principles should be followed?
Rules	What specific rules should guide us?
Concrete judgments	What is mandated in a particular instance?

🖋🖋🖋 Group Discussion Questions

• How was it that Bill Clinton ("slick Willy") demolished George Bush Sr. when Bush tried to make character a campaign issue?

• Discuss the ways moral discussion can be spoken about by referring to the table in this chapter.

• Try to discuss examples for each section of the table. 🖋🖋🖋

27

Getting Where You Are Going: The Only Way to Go!

Observing the lives of people who have mastered adversity, I have noted that they have established goals and sought with all their effort to achieve them. From the moment they decide to concentrate all their energies on a specific objective, they began to surmount the most difficult odds.

Ari Kiev, author of *A Strategy for Daily Living*

This morning on my way to work I noticed a sign in a New York City subway car, boasting that New York City alone has roughly as many miles of subway tracks as the rest of the country combined. This impressive fact didn't seem to matter much when I realized that I had been so distracted by the sign that I missed the Bowling Green stop; the train was rapidly heading east to Brooklyn. Yikes! Fortunately, I was able to reverse direction at the next stop, and got to work on time. Unfortunately, the same is not the case with other types of "mistaken directions" in life.

Ironically, we usually carefully think about small matters, such as getting to work on time every day: When do I have to leave home? What is the quickest route? How do I avoid congestion? We have little patience for traffic or busses or trains that are delayed. But incredibly, when it comes to the larger question of the direction of our lives, many of us either ignore the matter or neglect it in favor of more immediate concerns. Even if we have long-range goals, all too often we don't pursue them faithfully.

> 🖉 🖉 🖉 **Question(s) to consider**: Do you have long-range goals? Do you review them? Do you keep them visible as a reminder to yourself? 🖉

The consequences of being distracted from long-term goals can be severe. The Five O'Clock Club encounters people every day who have been fixed on making money (under a variety of pressures), when they would have preferred to pursue their dreams, such as owning a small business, teaching, raising children, or going back to school for another degree. Without the proper sense of fulfillment, we can end up clinically depressed, medicated, and confused, with our personal lives in turmoil; and, at the very least, we experience early burnout.

In a study (reported in the *New York Times*, February 2, 1999), Dr. Richard Ryan, a professor of psychology at the

University of Rochester, found that people who primarily seek riches are more likely to be depressed and have more behavioral and physical problems than those who pursue their (other) long-term goals. Those with goals more closely tied to deeper human aspirations tend to be mentally and physically healthier. Ryan concludes that our culture is built precisely on those values detrimental to mental health. Clearly, all goals are not created equal.

The Five O'Clock Club solution to "going in the wrong direction" begins with the Fifteen- or Forty-Year Vision® (see the Appendix). Using this exercise, we ask clients to imagine themselves five, ten and fifteen years from now—then well into the future. With their visions in mind, people can take appropriate steps now to make them come true. Newcomers to The Club are often skeptical and want to skip this exercise, but we urge them to trust us on this one: Thousands of our clients have found the Forty-Year Vision® empowering.

It is simply a fact of life that we must make choices. We can't decide to pursue $250,000 per year, and fulfill a deeper desire to be a teacher. We can't work 60-hour weeks to make it on Wall Street and be home for our children. When we know what we really want, other things must be considered distractions or temptations.

So, pay as much attention to your life direction as you do to your commute. It's never too late. Get in touch with your deeper aspirations, and aim to reach the professional goals that are most fulfilling for you.

It is better by noble boldness to run the risk of being subject to half of the evils we anticipate than to remain in cowardly listlessness for fear of what may happen.

Herodotus

✒✒✒ Group Discussion Questions

• Why is it that being distracted from long-term goals can be severe?

• Why does the Five O'Clock Club have the "Seven Stories" exercise (in the appendix)? ✒✒✒

28

Targeting: The Truth Is Out There

We find ourselves not independently of other people and institutions but through them. We never get to the bottom of our selves on our own. We discover who we are face-to-face and side-by-side with others in work, love, and learning.

Robert N. Bellah, *et al.,* "Habits of the Heart"

You may be familiar with the old television series, "The X Files," in which the two star investigators search for evidence to prove or disprove the existence of extra-terrestrials. The search involves going to many places, meeting many people, and asking many questions. The investigators seek evidence based on real-world experience, and they listen carefully to people. This team is scientific about the search: they know that "the truth is out there" and they follow a trusted method to find it.

Your search for the proper direction in your life is much like that, although the proper direction is usually easier to find than extra-terrestrials (however, this doesn't always seem to be the case!). The proper approach, of course, is The Five O'Clock Club methodology: It is not enough to speculate or conjecture about where you might fit in personally and professionally—that's only the starting point. Once you have identified those things that you enjoy doing and do well and have also developed a vision for your future (see the Appendix)The Five O'Clock Club urges you to go to many places, meet many people, and ask many questions. The extrovert will find this easier than the introvert, but it doesn't matter; everyone must do it.

When you meet with people, you must ask the right questions. One of the best ones is, "What do you enjoy the most about (what you do, where you live – or whatever)." Also ask, "What do you enjoy the least?" These open-ended questions help you hear what is really going on. Learn to listen – really listen – and not "lead the witness," as they say in law. Probe and ask more questions to better understand what is going on and to determine if that direction is right for you. Good goals and extra-terrestrials have some things in common: Both tend to be pesky and elusive little entities that are often not where you expect to find them.

> *✐✐✐* **Question(s) to consider**: Sometimes, it's easier to think about the *answer* you want to find out than the *question* you ask. Not only think about what you want to know, but also how best to pose the query to someone else. Don't

make it a million–dollar question; a hundred–dollar question
is easier to answer. 🖊

Over time, you will become more skilled at listening to people, and adjusting your goals. If you fail to do this, you can waste a lot of time on the wrong ones. A client at The Club, whom we'll call John, finally admitted to his hard-headedness. He had one particular target in mind that wasn't working. It was difficult for him to get appointments with people because of his education and experience. The meetings he did manage to get didn't lead to others. When he asked, "If you had an opening right now, would you consider hiring a person like me?," the answers were usually negative—but he was ignoring the message. It was not until a career coach debriefed him in detail that it became clear that he wasn't listening. His search did not pick up steam until he finally developed the appropriate targets.

You will eventually find real-world goals that are right for you. But there are many potential places to live and work, and the labor market is changing rapidly. The only way to deal with a moving target is to constantly adjust your aim. You need to get out, listen to many people, and learn. The truth is quite literally out there.

*Every great personal victory was preceded
by a personal goal or dream.*

Dennis R. Webb

✐✐✐ Group Discussion Questions

• Can one find out the truth about self without contact with others? Explain.

• Why does the Five O'Clock Club say that individuals must position themselves for the long run? ✐✐✐

29

Be on Track— and the Right Track

A Reminder from Islam

If you look at yourself on the level of historical time, as a tiny but influential part of a century-long process, then at least you can begin to know your own address. You can begin to sense the greater pattern, and feel where you are within it, and your acts take on meaning.

Michael Ventura, as quoted by Peter Schwartz
in *The Art of the Long View*

A Forty-Year Vision®

The Five O'Clock Club recommends that you do your Fifteen- or Forty-Year Vision (see the Appendix) so you can get your whole life operating in the same direction. We recommend that you select the right track for you—and stay on it. Our mantra is, "Does this thing that you are considering fit in with your Forty-Year Vision? If not, DON'T DO IT!"

In the twenty-five years of The Club's existence nationally, we have heard a variety of stories from our clients about their Forty-Year Visions:

- A young man dropped the woman he was dating because, as glamorous as she was, he saw in his Forty-Year Vision that he wanted someone who would be more supportive and down-to-earth, and hold more compatible religious beliefs.

- Another Five O'Clock Clubber decided NOT to search internationally—even though most of his career had been abroad—because His Forty-Year Vision told him that he actually desired more stability (not money) and did not want to move his family around.

- A woman who had never been married or had had children, and was not even dating someone, could not expect to find someone who was right for her if she also took a new job that required seventy-hour weeks. She had to act with courage for her true vision.

Hence, the Forty-Year Vision is NOT and cannot be just about your career. It is impossible to just say, "Here is where I want my career to go," without also considering other aspects of your life. The beauty of the Forty-Year Vision is that it takes everything into consideration, as well as the fact that goals do in fact sometimes clash, and require hard choices.

Islam: Keeping Lives on Track

Islam sheds light on this kind of problem. Why not call upon the wisdom of Islam, since we have already looked to Buddhism and the Judeo-Christian tradition, with respect to other questions?

Islam is inextricably entwined with Judaism and Christianity. Adam, Noah, Abraham, Isaac, Jacob, Joseph, Job, Moses, David, Solomon, John the Baptist, and Jesus are all revered by the Islamic sacred scriptures, the Koran. According to Islam, God's (Allah's) final message to man was revealed to the prophet Mohammad and is consistent with all that had been said before.

Worthy Tracks for Ali and Sadat: Peace Making

The main lesson for us all from Islam flows from its strict monotheism: We must keep our lives in line with a larger over-arching track. There are two components to this. One is simply to have a track, and the other is to be sure it is a worthy one. We would all do well to keep what is truly important before our eyes. This is actually in keeping with Five O'Clock Club's philosophy. The Club recommends taking only that job that advances you toward your ultimate long-term goal.

As 2001 was rung in, it was heartening to see boxing great Mohammad Ali with the then New York City Mayor Rudolph Giuliani pressing the button on New Year's Eve, sending the crystal-covered ball on its ritual descent. One cannot help reflecting on the greatness of the man, who has been called the World's Greatest Athlete, and the overriding role of Islam in his life. Mohammad Ali has made it his track to teach people to treat each other with dignity and respect.

Anwar Sadat, another devout Muslim man of peace also comes to mind. Sadat was president of Egypt in the 1970s; he was *Time* magazine's Man of the Year in 1977; and winner of the Nobel peace prize in 1978 (he gave the money to the poor over the objections of his wife). Sadat, Israeli Prime Minister Menachem Begin, and President Carter signed the Camp David peace agreement, on March 26, 1979. What a breathtaking sight that was: the most prominent (political) representatives of Islam, Judaism, and Christianity together signing a peace agreement.

In 1996, Madame Jehan Sadat, Sadat's widow, described her husband and Islam this way:

Islam has been judged by images ever since some (radical) Iranian students held American diplomats hostage. Yet Islam is a religion based upon peace, love and compassion.

A religion that abhors violence and killing; upholding the sanctity of life is an obligation of all Muslims. Forgiveness for personal injuries is enjoined. Therefore, revenge and blood feuding are serious sins. And killing is one of the greatest sins. My husband was a devout Muslim who followed the teaching of Islam and lived by the words of the prophet Mohammad.

One point I wish to stress is that Islam is not just a religion, as religion is commonly understood in the West. It is a total way of life encompassing the entirety of man's existence; not separating the spiritual from the material, the religious from the secular. It is a divine system governing man's life by setting the rules and the standards for living.

Presentation on
"Religion and World Peace: A Muslim's View,"
Madame Jehan Sadat, April 18, 1996,
the Tanenbaum Center for Interreligious Understanding,
New York

🖋️🖋️🖋️ **Question(s) to consider**: Here's a really difficult question: What is your way of life? What track are you on? Are you driven by money? Comfort? Security? Caring for your family? One way to find an answer is doing the Forty-Year Vision. Once you have done this exercise, look back and see if you could summarize your vision in one sentence—it could be a long sentence! And it should contain the essential that drives you. 🖉

Misconceptions about Islam

Unfortunately, there is sometimes a profoundly negative view of Islam (it means "submission to God") in the popular American press. The national press especially scorns Islam, not only for highly publicized acts of violence perpetrated by a few, but also because Islam refuses to separate religion and practical life. A practicing Muslim actually believes in something. Gasp!

But this call not to separate religion from practical life is actually common to Islam's sibling religions, Judaism and Christianity. Madame Sadat perhaps did not realize this, since the separation of faith and practice is too often the case in the daily lives of Jews and Christians as opposed to doctrine (teaching).

Mohammad and Islam: A Strong Ethical Agenda

Mohammad was born in Mecca in 570 A.D., orphaned in childhood and brought up by his uncle. He married a rich widow (Khadija) and became a merchant. He was disturbed about the sad condition of his people, many of whom were ignorant, superstitious, drunken, dishonest, and so on. His ethical concerns eventually brought him to teach a new religion in secret at Mecca. This new religion was based on his spiritual experiences alone in the mountains. He became convinced that there was only one God, whom he called Allah, and that idolatry was the chief problem.

Mohammad's concern about the condition of his people gave Islam the strong ethical agenda that has endured to this day. Ignorance, superstition, drunkenness and dishonesty really stem from idolatry—putting something else higher in one's priorities than God—and can be avoided if the faithful Muslim follows the one God. There will be a Day of Judgment, which makes our daily conduct all the more important. We will be held accountable for keeping our lives "on the right track."

Conclusion

Properly harnessed, one can certainly see how the Islamic perspective can govern worklife in a favorable way, from which we might all learn. Islam reminds us of the importance of the following:

- Ethical action is important in any job—honesty, sobriety, hard work, and certainly discipline.

To deny this leads to frustration and burnout. This is a warning to workaholics to give up some of their controlling nature.

· Most importantly, work and act in a manner consistent with your core beliefs, your Forty-Year Vision, and your desires throughout life. Follow your vision of what is good, and accept the consequences.

· We may all have differences in the way we articulate our Forty-Year Vision. However, we can learn from Islam that any long-term vision should be a worthy one, and that it should be followed faithfully and with seriousness.

✒✒✒ Group Discussion Questions

• Are all representatives of Islam given to violence? (discuss Sadat's speech in this chapter.)

• What does a strong ethical dilemma have to do with the founding of Islam and behavior today? ✒✒✒

30

An Approach to New Year's Resolutions

Few things are impossible to diligence and skill.

Samuel Johnson, "A Dissertation on the Art of Flying"

$\mathcal{M}$ost of us want to better our lives and ourselves, and many of us make New Year's resolutions to that end. We resolve to exercise, eat less and lose weight, break a bad habit (e.g., smoking), pray regularly, mend relationships, and so forth. Unfortunately, many times, perhaps most of the time, we are unable to follow through. If you're like most of us, you have a hard time even remembering what your resolutions are. So this section is a brief "how to" lesson on resolutions for all those who want to do better. You'll recognize The Five O'Clock Club approach here.

Assessing

Carefully assess what it is that you want to accomplish. We recommend two strategies:

1. Don't take on so much that you don't accomplish anything.

2. Select the most important goals and accomplish them first.

Trying to do too many difficult things at once is a recipe for failure. It's much better to be realistic and tackle only the more-important tasks. For example, mending a broken relationship is probably more important than losing five pounds. Being on time for work is more important than organizing your sock drawer. If you follow this tip, you're much less likely to find yourself overwhelmed.

Targeting

When you formulate your goals (or targets), be as specific as possible. For example, don't just resolve to "be more organized" or to "lose weight" or "rebuild old relationships." Write down precisely what it is that you intend to organize. So you should write: *I will organize my garage; I will skip dessert twice a week; I will take my sister out to lunch once a month, since we have not seen each other in over a year;* and so on.

Planning

Major goals require a plan. If you decide to "organize your garage," you should list the steps it takes to do this and complete them one by one. For example, an incremental approach might look like this:

1. I will organize the major mechanical devices this Saturday. The lawn mower, snow blower, hedge clippers, and so on, will be in order.

2. The next Saturday: I will organize the tool drawers so that things are found easily.

3. The next Saturday: I will organize the section of the garage used for storage—throwing out items that are no longer wanted or needed.

4. The next Saturday: Now that things are in order, I will improve the aesthetic appeal by cleaning, hanging pictures, washing windows, and so on.

5. The first Saturday of every month, I will spend one hour keeping the garage in good order.

Significant goals will usually require that you break them down into steps. If you do this, you will be more likely to see progress and success.

Perhaps your goal is to "improve yourself professionally." The steps might look like this:

1. I will join the professional associations in my field.

2. I will volunteer for committees or leadership roles in these associations.

3. I will renew my membership in The Five O'Clock Club to keep up on career-management and job-search techniques.

4. I will seek assignments at work that challenge me and help me to grow professionally.

Writing, Reading—and Patience

Writing down your resolutions helps to solidify your thoughts and intentions. Beyond that, it reminds you what you have promised yourself to do. Keep the written resolutions somewhere so that you will see them daily. You might put your resolutions on the refrigerator door, in your locker at the gym, on your computer monitor, and add them to your " to do" list. Above all, read your resolutions regularly, and don't be too hard on yourself. All is not lost if you backslide (e.g., you fail to skip desserts one week)—but don't wait until next year to try again. And so what if you think of a great resolution on January 15th—the New Year is only a couple of weeks old. It's never too late.

Add a bit of willpower to all of the above, and you're well on your way to making some life changes in the New Year.

✐ ✐ ✐ Group Discussion Questions

- Why might *writing* resolutions help you keep them?

✐ ✐ ✐

31

Is My Potential Employer Ethical?

Research is the process of going up alleys to see if they are blind.

Marston Bates

*W*orking for an organization is not unlike a marriage: You want to associate with a partner of good character. How do you know if this is so? The time to find out about the ethics of the organization is during the job search process. As a job seeker, you need to do certain things to learn whether or not ethics is or is not part of the corporate culture. What can you do to learn about the role of ethics in the organization?

🖉🖉🖉 **Question(s) to consider:** In reading this chapter, you can put together *an ethics plan*. Tips are given here on how to mine the right information. Your plan can be simple: What are the ethical concerns important to you? Write them down on a 3x5 card. Then when you do your research you'll have a clearer focus of what you want to know most. 🖉

The job seeker should *ask everyone* about what it's like to work there. Ask in the men's (women's) room, ask the receptionist while you're waiting, and listen carefully. You'll get the truth, sometimes euphemistically, but you should be able to connect the dots. You might learn about the work/life balance at the company. Do you have to kiss your family goodbye to work there?

Ask *competitors* what they think of your potential new employer. Usually, another company will acknowledge the spirit of competition existing between them, but be able to say good things, as well. Ask around at trade association meetings to get an idea about the company's reputation. Listen to anyone who is *in the industry.*

Perhaps you can speak with a *former employee* of the company. You might be able to network into meeting such a person—perhaps even the person you're replacing.

Read the *news!* If you're thinking about going to work for a large employer, the chances are high that it is in the news from time to time. Of course, any company scandals (such as in the cases of Enron and Arthur Anderson) can tell you a lot. Fortunately, most companies never make the news this way. But you can read the news about the company more subtly; do the company's practices seem exemplary or even ethically visionary?

The *Internet* is also a great source for information, including things relating to a company's ethics. Hoovers.com gives basic financial information about a company and tells who the major competitors are. Vault.com provides inside information about what it's really like to work for a particular company. Even Yahoo! has bulletin boards dedicated to the discussion of various industries. Read and ask questions on these bulletin boards and then carefully interpret what you read back.

Does the *hiring manager* give you any clues about the organization's ethics? If you are offered $95,000 salary and given an exaggerated expense account of $35,000, then this can be a fraudulent way of upping your salary. If you ask about severance, does the hiring manager make excessive promises without looking at the actual policy or checking with somebody? If you are offered $90,000 annually and are casually promised two years of severance in case of loss of job, you must ask yourself where the company controls and oversight are.

The hiring manager or HR representative, may tell you interesting things. She may comment on the organization's dealings with its competitors. Does she and others you meet gossip about competitors, make disparaging remarks about the competition's product, organization, or future? Do they tell you how cleverly they got rid of somebody? Judge their overall attitude toward acting upright in any matter that comes up for discussion.

✎✎✎ Group Discussion Questions

• Do the hiring manager and HR representative give you clues about the ethics of an organization? How? Name a few examples. ✎✎✎

32

When to Blow the Whistle

    mployees are sometimes presented with a difficult problem: Do I report an ethical lapse by my employer, or do I remain silent and say nothing? To whistle blow or not is the question. The Sarbanes-Oxley law both requires and protects "blowing the whistle" when there is wrong-doing.

For example, an engineer may detect a safety problem in the design of an automobile. Let's say that if there is even a minor crash, there is a slight probability of the fuel line's rupturing and causing a fire or explosion. Human lives could be at stake, so our engineer goes to his superiors with the hope that they will listen to him and act appropriately. However, he is told that it is unlikely (but certainly not impossible) that the line would rupture. He estimates that redesigning and changing the manufacturing process would be costly, and the company would rather avoid the lost time and money. Should the engineer blow the whistle and contact the press, or the government regulators?

Safety issues can occur with the design and manufacture of almost anything, including cars, busses, trains, toys, electric appliances, and airplanes. Other issues also raise the question of whistle blowing: A business with a manufacturing plant can produce byproducts that pollute the environment. If this pollution is in excess of what is allowed by regulations, should the employee speak up or remain silent?

These situations are always complicated by the danger to the employee's legitimate self-interest. The employer could very well mistreat the employee after the whistle has been blown. Often times, the employee is seen as disloyal, a loudmouth, and a danger to the welfare of the organization. Indeed, the single event could have implications for the employee's entire career.

> *🖉🖉🖉* **Question(s) to consider:** Do you know someone outside of the organization whom you can bounce your ideas off? She doesn't have to be a lawyer, just someone you trust who has good common sense. *🖉*

With lives and careers at stake, we need to have some method of thinking about this ethical problem on whistle blowing; the table on the following page does just that. The process absolutely must begin with the FACTS. Without the proper facts, more damage can be done than good. One could jeopardize one's entire career over mistaken information. The issue must impact the common good and be significant

enough to justify whistle blowing. All other methods of resolution must be tried and exhausted before doing something
as dramatic as whistle blowing. It is, of course, preferable if
the in-house managers take the appropriate action without
external coercion. Since anonymous tips are rarely believed
and trusted, ideally the employee would take responsibility for
his/her whistle blowing.

You might some day be presented with this difficult problem: to whistle blow or not. These four criteria could make
your life easier, since they offer a way to think and act about
the problem. With these criteria and other things in mind, follow your best judgment.

The Matter at Hand	Criteria
Get the facts	The employee must be absolutely certain of all the facts. This will involve research and speaking to other people. Be sure to keep records and preserve evidence.
The issue	The problem must involve a significant ethical lapse.
Other means	The employee must first attempt an orderly in-house resolution of the problem. The employee should visit the appropriate supervisors, managers, and executives to see if an internal solution to the problem is possible.
Responsibility	Since anonymous tips are rarely believed and trusted, ideally, the employee would take responsibility for his/her whistle blowing.

✐✐✐ Group Discussion Questions

- Name the hierarchy of people in an organization who might confront people about an ethical lapse.

- Is maximizing freedom always a good idea? ✐✐✐

33

How to Terminate Employees While Respecting Human Dignity

"There is nothing worse than being escorted from your place of
work, a place where you have come day after day and given your
time and your blood. You missed your kid's soccer games to be
there, and now they are saying to you, 'You are so dangerous that
you must be escorted from this place. We paid you a salary, we gave
you a 401K contribution, we gave you health benefits, we gave you
vacation and now today, all of a sudden, you are so awful that we
have to remove you as if you were a criminal.'

"Escorting someone out should be reserved for situations in which,
if you did not escort the person out, you would be placing the rest of
your staff in jeopardy. The circumstances are so rare in which you
would need to do that. If an employee threatens to kill people,
that's the one who needs to be escorted out."

Denise Z. Kaback, Director, Human Resources,
at the law firm Schulte Roth & Zabel LLP

ᵍ ᵍ ᵍ **Question(s) to consider**: A theme that runs through this chapter is "being a good person." See how this theme underlies the steps that follow. *ᵍ*

Termination with dignity helps both the employee and the organization move forward.
   · Have you ever had to dismiss someone?
   · Have you ever been dismissed yourself?
   · How was it handled?
   · Could it have been done better?

Overview: A Kind Word Helps

If you lay off one or more staff members, what impact will that have on those who remain? Will productivity—and the bottom line—suffer? Are you likely to lose your best people who will worry about their positions? Or will morale increase, because you handled the terminated employees with dignity?

This chapter can help. Here is what will be covered:
   · Allow separated employees a decompression period in familiar surroundings. Let them have some control over how they leave. If possible, let them finish tasks they want to finish and make arrangements for keeping in touch with coworkers.
   · A kind word helps during the dismissal meeting.

- Give your employees the kind of outplacement that gives them dignity while positioning them for the future.

The central idea of this chapter is this: The separation should be handled such that both the employee and the organization are empowered to move forward.

Part I: The Case for Termination with Dignity

Whatever the reason for the separation, few workplace situations are dreaded more than a face-to-face meeting to break the news that an employee is being dismissed. It is not uncommon that the person losing the job has little idea of what's coming—and in all too many cases, unfortunately, the manager has little training in how to handle the situation. We must recognize the difficult business and human problems that involuntary termination presents.

Organizations need a termination policy that would apply in all but the most extreme circumstances.

Regrettably, the termination process is given far less attention than the hiring process. But there has been a trend in the last few years to correct this imbalance—for the very simple reason that there is much more built-in turbulence in the workplace than there was only a few decades ago. The average American today has been in his or her job for only four years, and, not surprisingly, expects to be in that job for only those four years.

Separations due to downsizings, mergers, relocations, and closings are now part of the landscape. Terminations for cause can be on a continuum ranging from an employee's inability to adapt to a new computer system to those situations in which other employees or the organization are put at risk. Although it makes great sense to handle potentially violent or otherwise risk-filled situations with caution, it makes no sense to handle all employees as if they were a threat. Organizations need termination policies that apply in all but the most egregious circumstances, assuring that:

- The goodwill toward the organization stays intact.
- The remaining employees feel secure.
- The leaving employee(s) feel empowered.

If for no other reason than the good of the workplace itself—the effect that separations have on those who remain—it would be foolhardy to act as if the exit phase of employment doesn't deserve major attention.

Today, organizations are faced with an increasingly competitive labor market. It may be more difficult in the long run to recruit workers, as well as keep up productivity, in an organization that fails to treat its workers with dignity.

Employment in this country is for the most part "at the pleasure of" both parties. Organizations—with some restrictions—can hire and fire at will. However, every employee deserves to be terminated with *dignity*. We have chosen that term after careful consideration. No less a body than the United Nations speaks of treating humans with *dignity*, especially in critical situations.

Employees are clearly resources and they contribute to productivity, but unlike facilities and equipment, humans have intrinsic worth beyond their contribution to the organization. Our goal here is to identify practices that benefit the parties involved, both employee and employer. Put yet another way: The termination should be handled such that both the employee and the organization *are empowered to go forward*.

Progress in this area has been uneven; American leadership should devote increasing attention, energy, and dollars to refining and improving the separation process. And while organizations are looking at this issue more closely, mostly because of mergers and downsizings, separation with dignity should apply to *all* situations: the employee who is let go because of poor job performance is no less entitled to decent and respectful treatment consistent with the facts of each situation than someone who is terminated just because of downsizing. Even in the case of an employee's being discharged for willful misconduct, decency should not be suspended.

Why Should the Employer Care?

1. **Termination with dignity increases the organization's ability to hire the right people.** An organization's ability to attract the best talent is influenced by its goodwill in the marketplace, which depends to some extent on how it handles terminated employees.

    The workplace today is circular, not linear. Employees don't come in and stay. They come and go and intermix with people outside who learn how they were treated. When an organization lets someone go, that person touches dozens of others who influence the company's image—and its ability to hire—in the marketplace. If an organization wants to compete and hire well, it must give attention to the way it lets people go.

2. **Termination with dignity is becoming a routine part of doing business in a civilized society.** Not too many decades ago, few practical business people could have been persuaded that the routine cost of business included offering employees paid vacations, health and dental insurance coverage, personal days, matching contributions to pension plans, and so forth. Over time, organizational thinking has changed, in part based on the recognition that employees are re-

sources for which there is an increasingly competitive market.

Unlike facilities and equipment, humans have intrinsic worthbeyond their present contribution to the organization.

The costs of developing and implementing digni-fied termination policies should be considered a part of doing business in a civilized society. Dignified ter-mination should be seen as one of many "benefits" provided by the employer. The movement in the re-cently past century toward expanding and increasing employee benefits reflects an understanding of the "social contract" or "social covenant"—accepted standards as to what is decent for ordinary working men and women. One of the major components of our social covenant as Americans, as fellow citizens wishing to enjoy the benefits of a vigorous economy, is the understanding that we are obliged to contribute to the *general well-being.*

As termination with dignity becomes a standard in the workplace, organizations that fail to practice it run the risk of damaging their reputations.

Hence, we have no trouble arguing for compassionate termination policies that reduce stress on families, lessen financial hardships, and decrease the chances that discharged employees will suffer emotional crises. These topics are elaborated on in the sidebar.

3. **Termination with dignity protects corporate profitability.** Such termination policies do, in fact, protect corporate profitability. Shareholder value will increase and business will profit in the long run by moving vigorously in this direction. At least two arguments can be advanced here:

   a. **Organizations do not welcome negative publicity.** Notoriety is not good for business, for example, product recalls, boardroom scandals, headlines about embezzlement—or news that 20 executives have been cut from the payroll just three months short of their retirement benefits. An organization's good name is an asset not to be squandered. And organizations do acquire reputations as bad places to work, because of poor benefits or a general perception about the way people are treated. Organizations that earn a reputation for decency in the way they let people go are considered attractive places for competent people to work. As termination with dignity becomes standard in the workplace, organizations that fail to practice it run the risk of damaging their reputations.

b. **The impact on the productivity of the remaining employees is important.** The morale of the employees who survive a downsizing—or, for that matter, witness a single separation-for-cause—should be a primary concern to management. Major layoffs typically result in increased workloads for the remaining employees, which is cause enough for stress and hard feelings. But many factors can come into play: those who are left behind can feel a loss because familiar faces are suddenly gone, teams are broken up, and officemates have disappeared. There can be anger that "things aren't the way they used to be," and fear that the same fate may be in store for those who remain.

Preparedness entails

- Guidelines for management's behavior on the day of termination.
- Trained managers.
- Carefully prepared (though flexible) positive scripts.
- Plans for taking care of separated employees (including quality monetary packages).
- A full description of career coaching and other services ready to distribute.
- A list of each employee's contributions and strong points that have been valued over the years.
- Thought regarding the method of severance payout.

Termination with dignity does, in fact, *protect* corporate profitability. The reputation of the organization and employee morale are protected. Shareholder value will increase and business will profit in the long run by moving vigorously in this direction.

Resentment and fear can be eased if there is a general perception that the separated employees got a fair deal and that management handled the terminations in a decent and caring fashion. It is in management's interest that:

- People still believe that this is a good place to work.
- Employee energy and focus are put into work and productivity.
- Venting and complaining be kept to a minimum.

Employees who have witnessed termination with dignity will be more inclined to like the organization and support its goals and mission.

There is a growing awareness in the American workforce that mergers and staff reductions are now an inevitable part of the corporate landscape. This should be accompanied by a growing awareness that management will merge and cut with care for human dignity; that it is committed to making the termination as painless as possible and to protecting the well-being of employees as productive resources.

The costs of developing and implementing dignified termination policies should be considered a part of doing business correctly in a civilized society.

Part II: How to Terminate With Dignity

In those few cases where the former employee has taken legal action, the reasons for doing so usually revolve around treatment during the termination meeting.

Therefore, during the meeting, consider the following:
- The employee wants to know what went wrong.

People are more likely to be able to go forward if they are given an explanation.

- The employee is listening for a kind word about past performance.
- There is the matter of pride: How will the departure be portrayed to the remaining workforce?
- There are the pragmatics: How am I going to survive? Have available, full written summaries of severance benefits prepared with as much care as the benefit booklets handed to new hires.
- Discuss other issues, such as professional references, so the employee can formulate a strategy to move forward.
- Allow people to return to familiar surroundings and share reactions with friends—to proceed with some degree of normalcy for the time being. This is part of the empowering process.

Before, During and After the Termination Meeting

Proper termination is a lengthy process. Many factors come into play, so it's helpful to analyze the method *chronologically*. To carry it off well, pay attention to the:

- Extensive groundwork required beforehand.
- Protocols and procedures to be followed when it happens.

- Appropriate actions required in the days, weeks, or even months after a layoff or termination.

Before the Meeting

Impulse, or "letting the chips fall where they may," has no role in affirming and constructing a proper termination policy. Because preparedness is vital, termination procedures must be imbedded in a written policy and, over time, instilled in the organization's culture. These practices must become a part of workplace protocols. In other words, this is not something to be put on the shoulders of untutored managers. The organization's guiding philosophy on the issue must be studied and mastered.

Letting people go is an extraordinarily important and sensitive task. Those entrusted with this responsibility should be trained to handle the termination process.

Managers Must Be Trained

When people are going through a termination process, all parties are moving into the arena of human hurt: great sensitivity will be required. Human lives and futures are at stake and the organization's image is on the line. Accordingly, managers and HR officers must be trained to listen attentively and to respond to human distress.

Preparedness for this role may require, at the very least, attendance at seminars, tutoring by specially trained HR officers, and scripts.

Enlightened organizations have long trained managers to improve their hiring and interviewing skills. This enables them to be more astute in selecting candidates and more aware of legal pitfalls: Who needs a manager who hasn't gotten the word that a female candidate can't be asked blatantly sexist questions? The same degree of training should be given to managers for the hard task of letting people go: Who needs a manager who is too busy to care about feelings and just wants to get the unpleasant business behind him—or worse, who views his task as an opportunity to settle scores? *Letting people go* is an extraordinarily important and sensitive matter. Those entrusted with this responsibility should have the benefit of professional coaching. Smaller organizations could at least give their managers selected reading material or perhaps this chapter.

Preparedness is the key factor to ensure that the financial and emotional well-being of the terminated employee are protected.

Develop Positive Scripts

Carefully prepared (though flexible), positive scripts are indispensable to the separation process. Enabling people to pick up the pieces and move on should be the goal; separated employees who have been emotionally battered and damaged by the termination process may be ill-equipped to grapple with the emotional battering that may come next (i.e., a job search). Saying a nice word plays a critical role; the lack of kind words eats at people and erodes morale. The guiding norm, at the very least, should be "to do no harm." In a downsizing or merger, it is easier to assure people that this is a *no-fault situation,* but even here self-esteem can take a beating and positive scripts are essential.

The employee is listening for a kind word about past performance, such as:

- "George, you've been a trooper. You've helped us for 15 years and I'm sorry that the organization has moved in a different direction."
- "Mary, you have excellent people-relations skills and have added a lot to the group."

Termination procedures must be imbedded in written policy and instilled in the organizational culture. Otherwise, people won't want to work there again—or recommend that others do.

Point Out Each Employee's Strengths

The manager should be prepared to review, with each employee, his or her contributions and strong points that have been valued over the years. Even in a termination-for-performance, prompted by the fact that someone's skills were inadequate for a particular situation, the person's assets and abilities can still be acknowledged. A termination-for-performance should not be an occasion for abuse. As will be noted shortly, financial considerations are crucial, but a generous dollar settlement usually cannot erase bitter memories of uncaring or even unkind words. The "sharp stick in the eye" is likely to be remembered long after the separation money has been spent. Indeed, in those few cases in which former employees have taken legal action, the personal reasons for doing so usually have to do with the treatment during the separation process.

"The Package"

Preparedness also means creating plans for taking care of separated employees: An important element in enhancing a corporation's reputation is the quality of "the package." The quality of the package is measured by how much the person *is able to move forward* professionally and personally.

Termination with dignity presumes that the package will include:

- Severance pay.
- Professional support for finding a new position (i.e., career coaching and other such services).
- In-house counseling to help separated employees

come to an understanding of what combination of severance pay and support services is appropriate.

Carefully prepared (though flexible) positive scripts are an indispensable element of the process. For example, "George, you've been a trooper. I'm sorry that the organization has moved in a different direction."

Many employees will be unaware of the importance of various transitional support services, and may dismiss them in favor of cash settlements. However, management has an obligation to evaluate separated employees individually, and guide them with sensitivity, based upon their needs and histories. Organizations should devote time and care to reviewing individual profiles and needs to construct separation packages consisting of cash, career coaching, and other services in line with the organization's policies, usually in proportion to the employee's level and years of service.

Being prepared means having a full explanation of the termination services ready to hand to the employee—a detailed written explanation of benefits (i.e., career coaching help, office space, educational grants, health insurance continuation, and so on).

Smaller organizations often cannot afford extensive packages. When choices have to be made based on cost, it's usually best to provide employees with ongoing career coaching until they are re-employed (rather than, for example, short-term coaching along with expensive space and other support services).

Preparedness also means deciding upon how severance will be paid out. For example, except for special requests or circumstances, paying a six-month lump sum in November or December—and enormously inflating the W2 for the year—will certainly create resentment. Severance pay is rightly viewed as limited and precious: no more of it than absolutely necessary should be lost to taxes. The costs for bookkeeping and payroll services may be higher if the payout lasts for six months vs. one or two, but this should be done if it is in the best interest of the employee.

Information Sharing

While there may be no way to eliminate the element of surprise, there are ways to reduce shock and humiliation in the wake of a downsizing that has been a closely guarded secret. Except in the most unusual of circumstances, there is little justification for "sudden death" discharges; there are plenty of horror stories of fired employees who are asked to leave the building immediately, even by being escorted from their desks to the door by security. The person is treated as a threat. The trusted employee has suddenly become a danger. This certainly creates the impression that the termination is a punishment, causing humiliation and resentment. Too many managers think that this is simply the way to do it: "It's over, let's make a clean break."

Management must consider the consequences in each case. Most managers would resent an employee's failing to give two weeks' notice, while, of course, the dynamics can be vastly different when the separation is the employer's decision. Organizations should consider the positives of allowing for a decompression period, for an appropriate time in familiar surroundings, allowing discharged employees to finish tasks, complete projects, and make arrangements for keeping in touch with coworkers. This may strike some as being highly idealistic, but carrying it off depends on *how well the reason for the termination has been explained,* about which more will be said later.

There is little justification for "sudden death" discharges. These cause humiliation and resentment.

Attention should be given to the secrecy that usually surrounds merger negotiations or plans for downsizings. This subject is beyond the scope of this chapter, but it needs to be carefully analyzed because of its impact on the workplace. It's harder to achieve termination with dignity when people have little or no warning that jobs are about to be cut. There's a need for confidentiality at some level, but there's also a need to evaluate the impact of secrecy on the men and women in the workforce.

During the Meeting

The musical "A Chorus Line" is the story of young Broadway hopefuls trying out for a new production. Near the end of the show, after all have taken their turns at dance and song, they stand in a line on the stage nervously facing the director. He announces, "When I call your name, please step forward." Those called do so; smiles and looks of relief cross their faces. But after calling ten people forward, the director says to them, "Thank you for coming, we appreciate your trying out, but I'm sorry we can't use you. Those who remain will receive contracts in the mail." It was a particularly cruel way to announce his selection.

The quality of the package is measured by how much individuals are able to move forward professionally and personally.

The Delivery

Much depends on how people get the news—the words that are actually used are important—and on how the events of the day unfold. If it *seems* that the organization is acting cruel or mean, there can be significant harm—both to the individual and to the organization in the form of damaged reputation or even lawsuits. While almost all legal actions brought by terminated employees are unsuccessful—

employment law allows either the employer or employee to end the association at will—such actions remain a nuisance. Lawsuits are often emotional reactions to the hurt inflicted during the termination.

It's best, for example, if ten people are to be cut from a staff of forty-five, that either all ten are called to a special meeting or that the names of all ten are announced as closely together as possible. This is especially true if all forty-five are on the same floor or in the same department. The remaining thirty-five should be told what is happening. Sometimes, management doesn't think far enough ahead to see that this is the best course. On the other hand, when the announcements are spaced out too far, the atmosphere can become unbearable, ruining productivity, while dozens of people are dreading that the phone will ring. If a humane policy is in place, the discharged people can return to their desks when they are ready, discuss events and feelings with co-workers, and sit down for a helpful session with a career or other counselor.

Most managers would resent an employee's failing to give two weeks' notice. Yet, often, employees are simply ushered out the door.

When the time for a termination arrives—manager and employee are face-to-face—termination with dignity requires addressing the employee's needs on two levels. He or she has just received life-changing news and will likely be curious about two things:

- Why has this happened to me?
- What is going to happen to me now—how am I going to survive?

Horror stories abound of fired employees being asked to leave the building immediately, even being escorted by security from their desks to the door.

"Why Has This Happened to Me?"

"Why has this happened to me?," is an emotional, self-esteem question. Representatives of the organization should be prepared to explain, at least generally, why the organization is cutting staff, merging or closing; but they should be sensitive to feelings of the person being singled out. "How did I end up in the group being downsized?" This feeling may be expressed in a variety of ways—or not at all, in the turmoil of the moment—but the underlying plea is, "Please help me to understand what went wrong." As discussed earlier, representatives of the organization should be prepared with positive scripts tailored to each employee. People are more likely to feel empowered if they *do* understand what went wrong.

Since the primary rationale for termination with dignity is to empower people to move ahead with their

lives, putting in a good word for them can play a crucial role—and has been shown not to put the organization at risk.

Further, people's pride must be considered. Separated employees will need to know how their departure will be portrayed to the remaining staff; they should be assured that they will not come off looking like has-beens or part of a defective group that wasn't pulling its weight. Management can:

- Set the tone for the day.
- Preserve an atmosphere of respect.
- Convey genuine regret that organization had to make what is a hard decision.

"What is going to happen to me now? How am I going to survive?"

These questions are typically rooted in simple panic. A fair amount of people live from paycheck to paycheck, or, at the very most, may have no more than a few weeks or months of savings. Some may be in too much shock to absorb a detailed explanation of the terms of severance, but it is best to work on the assumption that survival information should be conveyed *immediately*.

Managers should give the employee full *written* statements of separation benefits and policies, that is, what the separated employee can expect in terms of:

- Money
- Career coaching services
- Office space, telephone, other such support
- Health coverage
- 401K rollovers
- Pension rights
- Compensation for earned vacation days
- References

These statements should be prepared with as much care as the benefit booklets handed to new hires, as already noted above.

Shock and panic can be reduced if people leave the manager's office with some sense that they are not really on the edge of disaster, that a support system has been put into place.

On-site Liaison

The HR staff should be assigned to liaise with separated workers. The primary message should be, "You have been an important and valued part of the team; we want to help you move on." This means a willingness to help people navigate life during the weeks and months that follow.

After the Meeting

References

Management should seriously consider the issue of references. Since the primary rationale for termination with dignity is to empower people and enable them to move ahead with their lives, *putting in a good word* for them can play a crucial role. Does maintaining a wall of silence help?

For years, organizations have believed that references can translate easily into lawsuits. So, most employers do little more than verify the dates of employment—and forbid managers to respond to requests for references. The result, of course, is that information is sought informally and travels by the grapevine—increasing the chances that hearsay or rumors can damage reputations and careers.

Offering references does not, however, put organizations at risk. *The New York Times* (February 21, 1999) reported the following:

> "According to C. Patrick Fleener, a management professor at Seattle University, 'the fear of being sued and losing is not well founded.' Professor Fleener, co-author of a study of Federal and state court records nationwide from 1965 to 1970 and 1985 to 1990, found only 16 defamation cases arising from reference checks. And plaintiffs prevailed in only 4 of the 16, he found."

It is worth the effort to reinvent strategies on references and convey good news about people to prospective employers. Even those who are fired for poor performance deserve to have their good points preserved in the record. This is consistent with the philosophy, "to do no harm." The policy should be that although today's events involve stress and a significant setback, the organization should act so that these feelings need not be any greater than necessary.

Making It a Reality

A thorough survey of the American employment landscape undoubtedly would reveal wide variations in termination policies; some organizations would get high marks, while others would be seen as brutal. Mostly, it seems that the standards advocated here are already accepted in theory by many, and even offered as written policy by some. Termination with dignity, however, is hard work, requiring a heavy commitment of money and human talent. Writing it up in the policy manual is one thing; true implementation is another. "Our employee manual was heavy with human concern," an executive noted in commenting on an especially bruising departmental layoff. But to save money in the short term, the guidelines were simply ignored.

Further study, research, and consultation among leading executives should be undertaken to consider *strategies for implementation:* How can ideas and ideals be translated into plans of action? Often, this means a significant change in an organization's culture. As was mentioned at the outset, many benefits are now taken for granted as part of the deal that American workers expect (e.g., insurance coverage and paid vacations). Termination with dignity should take its place as a benefit, along with others, to *maximize the effectiveness of the workforce and the development of employees as resources, as well as to respect our human dignity.* At present, the termination process is frequently *crippling* both to organizations and workers. Nothing in law or economics requires that this state of affairs be preserved.

HR managers are realizing that Five O'Clock Club outplacement is more effective and less expensive than conventional outplacement. The remaining employees feel better knowing that their fellow workers receive a full year of coaching help.

Conventional outplacement generally lasts only for a short period, and usually provides expensive office space, a phone, and a computer—but with limited coaching and outdated job-search techniques. Just about everyone today has a home computer, and either a printer or access to inexpensive printing and copying. There really isn't a need to give a laid off employee an office. What is needed are updated career coaching, support, and practice in the latest job-hunting techniques. That's The Five O'Clock Club method.

Based on twenty-five years of research, our cost-effective corporate packages include private coaching that far exceeds what traditional outplacement firms offer, as well as one full *year* of group coaching. That is—again in contrast to traditional outplacement firms—people may return to us if their new job or consulting assignment has not worked out.

An outplacement package can cost as little as $2,000. Our Premium package, for those earning over $100,000 per year, includes fourteen hours of private coaching, as well as one *year* of small-group coaching for only $5,000.

At traditional outplacement firms, people usually get three months of space and phones, but only five hours of coaching, the service job hunters need most. The quality of traditional outplacement has declined as coaches are overloaded with short-term clients, handling three times the caseload of previous years.

Separated Professionals and Managers Prefer The Five O'Clock Club

Time and again, The Five O'Clock Club is the provider of choice. In a recent downsizing of nineteen professionals and managers (whose salaries ranged from $35,000 to $150,000), all 19 were given a choice between The Five O'Clock Club and a major outplacement organization. Fourteen chose The Five O'Clock Club. We were able to offer eight hours of one-to-one coaching and one year of small group coaching, along with books, CDs, and other materials. The major outplacement firm was offering three- and six-month packages depending on seniority. Employees consistently choose expert career coaching over the space provided by traditional outplacement firms. Be sure to tell your friends and those in human resources about the most cost-effective job-search solution available.

🍃🍃🍃 Group Discussion Questions

· What does this mean: 'The separations should be handled such that both the employee and the organization are empowered to move forward."? How does this apply to a termination? Why is it so very important? How do we interpret "move forward?" Use the entire chapter to answer this.

· Can you add to the tables of preparedness ("Preparedness entails") and the following table ("In those few cases...")?

· Give hints on the proper manner of termination before the meeting, during the meeting, and after the meeting.

· The tables at the end of this chapter have both quotes and surprisingly similar versions of the Christian "golden rule." Take some time in evaluating the "Quotations to Inspire You" and "The Golden Rule." What surprises you the most? 🍃🍃🍃

Quotations to Inspire You

Difficult terminations and situations involving threatening employees are similar to other volatile social situations: . . . the interests of one party are in direct conflict with the interests of another party. Accordingly, resolutions that are completely satisfactory to all parties are rare.

To complicate matters, the difficult employee often has similar problems away from work as well. The good things in his life are like dominos that have started to topple: Confidence has toppled into performance, which topples into identity, which knocks over self-esteem. The loss of his job may knock over the few remaining dominos, but the one that employers must be careful not to topple is the dignity domino because when that falls, violence is most likely.

> Gavin DeBecker, "The Gift of Fear and Other Survival
> Strategies that Protect Us from Violence"

He means well, but he means well feebly.

> Theodore Roosevelt (speaking about a political rival)

Since college, I'd always worked at top speed. From a demanding law practice, I'd gone to work in Richard Nixon's White House. Days began at 6 A.M., and I seldom was home before ten at night. Suddenly there was a vacuum in my life. I had nothing productive to do.

> John Ehrlichman, former White House domestic
> policy coordinator, on losing his job

Time-limited contracts will become commoner. Executives have often been hired with contracts that specify some compensation if the arrangement is terminated sooner than planned, and such clauses will become available to other workers as well. All of us are going to move toward some kind of contract with the organizations that pay for our services.

William Bridges, "JobShift: How to Prosper
in a Workplace without Jobs"

Heroes come in all sizes, and you don't have to be a giant hero. You can be a very small hero. It's just as important to understand that accepting self-responsibility for the things you do, having good manners, caring about other people—these are heroic acts. Everybody has the choice of being a hero or not being a hero every day of their lives.

George Lucas, film director, as quoted in
Time magazine, April 26, 1999

To feel that one has a place in life solves half the problem of contentment.

George Edward Woodberry, American poet,
critic and educator (1855–1930)

The Golden Rule

Bahá'í: "And if thine eyes be turned towards justice, choose thou for thy neighbor that which thou choosest for thyself."

–Lawh'i'Ibn'i'Dhib, "Epistle to the Son of the Wolf", 30

Buddhism: "Hurt not others in ways you yourself would find hurtful."

–Udana-Varga, 5:18

Christianity: "In everything do to others as you would have them do to you; for this is the law and the prophets." *–Matthew, 7.12*

Confuscianism: "Do not unto others what you do not want them to do to you." *–Analects, 15.13*

Hinduism: "This is the sum of duty: do naught unto others which would cause you pain if done to you." *–The Mahabharata, 5:1517*

Islam: "Not one of you is a believer until he loves for his brother what he loves for himself." *–Fortieth Hadith of an-Nawawi, 13*

Jainism: "A man should wander about treating all creatures as he himself would be treated." *–Sutrakritanga, 1.11.33*

Judaism: "What is hateful to you, do not do to your neighbor: that is the whole of the Torah; all the rest of it is commentary."

–Talmud, Shabbat, 31a

Native American: "Respect for all life is the foundation."

–The Great Law of Peace

Sikhism: "Treat others as thou wouldst be treated thyself." *–Adi Granth*

Taoism: "Regard your neighbor's gain as our own gain and your neighbor's loss as your own loss." *–T'ai Shang KanYing P'ien*

Zoroastrianism: "That nature alone is good which refrains from doing unto another whatsoever is not good for itself." *–Dadistan-I-Dinik, 94:5*

Reprinted with permission of the Tanenbaum Center for Interreligious Studies, Union Theological Seminary in the City of New York

Appendix 1

Exercises to Analyze Your Past and Present: The Seven Stories Exercise

The direction of change to seek is not in our four dimensions: it is getting deeper into what you are, where you are, like turning up the volume on the amplifier.

Thaddeus Golas, *Lazy Man's Guide to Enlightenment*

In this exercise, you will examine your accomplishments, looking at your strongest and most enjoyable skills. The core of most coaching exercises is some version of the Seven Stories Exercise. A coach may give you lots of tests and exercises, but this one requires *work* on your part and will yield the most important results. An interest or personality test is not enough. There is no easy way. Remember, busy executives take the time to complete this exercise—if it's good enough for them, it's good enough for you.

Do not skip the Seven Stories Exercise. It will provide you with important information about yourself for the direction of your personal life as well as your career. If you're like most people, you have never taken the time to sort out the things you're good at and also are motivated to accomplish. As a result, you probably don't use these talents as completely or as effectively as you could. Too often, we do things to please someone else or to survive in a job. Then we get stuck in a rut—that is, we're *always* trying to please someone else or *always* trying to survive in a job. We lose sight of what could satisfy us, and work becomes drudgery rather than fun. When we become so enmeshed in survival or in trying to please others, it may be difficult to figure out what we would rather be doing.

When you uncover your motivated skills, you'll be better able to identify jobs that allow you to use them, and recognize other jobs that don't quite fit the bill. *Motivated skills* are patterns that run through our lives. Since they are skills from which we get satisfaction, we'll find ways to do them even if we don't get to do them at work. We still might not know what these skills are—for us, they're just something we do, and we take them for granted.

Tracking down these patterns takes some thought. The payoff is that our motivated skills do not change. They run throughout our lives and indicate what will keep us motivated for the rest of our lives.

Look at Donald Trump. He knows that he enjoys—and is good at—real estate and self-promotion, and that's what he concentrates on. You can identify commonalities in your accomplishments—aspects that you must have that will make you happier and more successful. In my case, for example, whether I was a computer programmer, a chief financial officer or a career coach, I've always found a way to teach others and often ran small groups – even in my childhood!

One's prime is elusive....You must be on the alert to recognize your prime at whatever time of life it may occur.

Muriel Spark, *The Prime of Miss Jean Brodie*

The Seven Stories Approach:

Background

This technique for identifying what people do well and enjoy doing has its roots in the work of Bernard Haldane, who, in his job with the U.S. government in the 1940s, helped military personnel transition their skills to civilian life. Its overwhelming success in this area won the attention of Harvard Business School where it went on to become a significant part of its Manual for Alumni Placement. Haldane's work is being carried on today all over the world through

DependableStrenghts.org. They have brought Haldane's method to places as diverse as South Africa and China, to colleges and universities and in their work with young people.

The Seven Stories (or enjoyable accomplishments) approach, now quite common, was taught to me by George Hafner, who used to work for Bernard Haldane.

The exercise is this: Make a list of all the enjoyable accomplishments of your life, those things you enjoyed doing *and also* did well. List at least 25 enjoyable accomplishments from all parts of your life: work, from your youth, your school years, your early career up to the present. Don't forget volunteer work, your hobbies and your personal life. Other people may have gotten credit or under-appreciated what you did. Or the result may not have been a roaring success. For example, perhaps you were assigned to develop a new product and take it to market. Let's say you worked on a project for two years, loved every minute of it, but it failed in the market. It doesn't matter. What matters is that you enjoyed doing it and did it well.

Examine those episodes that gave you a sense of accomplishment. You are asked to name 25 accomplishments so you will not be too judgmental—just list anything that occurs to you. Don't expect to sit down and think of everything. Expect to think of enjoyable accomplishments over the course of four or five days. Be sure to ask others to help you think of your accomplishments. Most people carry around a piece of paper so they can jot ideas down as they occur to them. When you have 25, select the seven that are most important to you by however you define important. Then rank them: List the most important first, and so on.

Starting with your first story, write a paragraph about each accomplishment. Then find out what your accomplishments have in common. If you are having trouble doing the exercises, ask a friend to help you talk them through. Friends tend to be more objective and will probably point out strengths you never realized.

You will probably be surprised. For example, you may be especially good interacting with people, but it's something you've always done and therefore take for granted. This may be a thread that runs through your life and may be one of your motivated skills. It *may* be that you'll be unhappy in a career that doesn't allow you to deal with people.

When I did the Seven Stories Exercise, one of the first stories I listed was from when I was 10 years old, when I wrote a play to be put on by the kids in the neighborhood. I rehearsed everyone, sold tickets to the adults for two cents apiece, and served cookies and milk with the proceeds. You might say that my direction as a *general manager*—running the whole show, thinking things up, getting everybody working together—was set in the fourth grade. I saw these traits over and over again in each of my stories.

After I saw those threads running through my life, it became easy for me to see the elements I must have in a career to be satisfied. When I would interview for a job or think of business ideas for myself (or when other people made suggestions), I could find out in short order whether the job or the business idea would address my motivated skills (running small groups, writing books, public speaking, and so on). If it didn't, I wouldn't be as happy as I could be, even though I may decide to take certain positions as an interim step toward a long-term goal. The fact is, people won't do as well in the long run in positions that don't satisfy their motivated skills.

Sometimes I don't pay attention to my own motivated skills, and I wind up doing things I regret. For example, in high school I scored the highest in the state in math. I was as surprised as everyone else, but I felt I finally had some direction in my life. I felt I had to use it to do something constructive. When I went to college, I majored in math. I almost flunked because I was bored with it. The fact is that I didn't enjoy math, I was simply good at it.

There are lots of things we're good at, but they may not be the same things we really enjoy. The trick is to find those things we are good at, enjoy doing, and feel a sense of accomplishment from doing.

To sum up: Discovering your motivated skills is the first step in career planning. I was a general manager when I was 10, but I didn't realize it. I'm a general manager now, and I love it. In between, I've done some things that have helped me toward my long-range goals, and other things that have not helped at all.

It is important to realize that the Seven Stories Exercise will not tell you exactly which career you should have, but the elements to look for in a career that you will find satisfying. You'll have a range to consider, and you'll know the elements you must have to keep you happy. Once you've selected a few career possibilities that might satisfy you, talk to people in those fields to find out if a particular field or industry is really what you want, and the possibilities for someone with your experience. That's one way to test if your aspirations are realistic.

After you have narrowed your choices down to a few fields with some possibilities that will satisfy your motivated skills, the next step is to figure out how to get there.

... be patient toward all that is unsolved in your heart and try to love the questions themselves like locked rooms and like books that are written in a foreign tongue.

Rainer Maria Rilke, *Letters to a Young Poet*

A Demonstration of the Seven Stories Exercise

To get clients started, I sometimes walk them through two or three of their achievement stories, and tell them the patterns I see. They can then go off and think of the seven or eight accomplishments they enjoyed the most and also performed well. This final list is ranked and analyzed in depth to get a more accurate picture of the person's motivated skills. I spend the most time analyzing those accomplishments a client sees as most important. Some accomplishments are more obvious than others. But all stories can be analyzed.

Here is Suzanne, as an example: "When I was nine years old, I was living with my three sisters. There was a fire in our house and our cat had hidden under the bed. We were all outside, but I decided to run back in and save the cat. And I did it."

No matter what the story is, I probe a little by asking questions: What was the accomplishment for you? and What about that made you proud? These questions give me a quick fix on the person.

The full exercise is a little more involved than this. Suzanne said at first: "I was proud because I did what I thought was right." I probed a little, and she added: "I had a sense of accomplishment because I was able to make an instant decision under pressure. I was proud because I overcame my fear."

I asked Suzanne for a second story; I wanted to see what patterns might emerge when we put the two together:

"Ten years ago, I was laid off from a large company where I had worked for nine years.

I soon got a job as a secretary in a Wall Street company. I loved the excitement and loved that job. Six weeks later, a position opened up on the trading floor, but I didn't get it at first. I eventually was one of three finalists, and they tried to discourage me from taking the job. I wanted to be given a chance. So I sold myself because I was determined to get that job. I went back for three interviews, said all the right things, and eventually got it."

What was the accomplishment?

What made her proud?

- "I fought to win."
- "I was able to sell myself. I was able to overcome their objections."
- "I was interviewed by three people at once. I amazed myself by saying, 'I know I can do this job.'"
- "I determined who the real decision maker was, and said things that would make him want to hire me."
- "I loved that job—loved the energy, the upness, the fun."

Here it was, 10 years later, and that job still stood out as a highlight in her life. Since then she'd been miserable and bored, and that's why she came to me. Normally after a client tells two stories, we can quickly name the patterns we see in both stories. What were Suzanne's patterns?

Suzanne showed that she was good at making decisions in tense situations—both when saving the cat and when interviewing for that job. She showed a good intuitive sense (such as when she determined who the decision maker was and how to win him over). She's decisive and likes fast-paced, energetic situations. She likes it when she overcomes her own fears as well as the objections of others.

We needed more than two stories to see if these patterns ran throughout Suzanne's life and to see what other patterns might emerge. After the full exercise, Suzanne felt for sure that she wanted excitement in her career, a sense of urgency—that she wanted to be in a position where she had a chance to be decisive and operate intuitively. Those are the conditions she enjoys and under which she operates the best.

Armed with this information, Suzanne can confidently say that she thrives on excitement, high pressure, and quick decision-making. And, she'll probably make more money than she would in *safe* environments. She can move her life in a different direction—whenever she is ready.

Pay attention to those stories that were most important to you. The elements in these stories may be worth repeating. If none of your enjoyable accomplishments were work related, it may take great courage to eventually move into a field where you will be happier.

People have to be ready to change. Fifteen years ago, when I first examined my own motivated skills, I saw possibilities I was not ready to handle. Although I suffered from extreme shyness, my stories—especially those that occurred when I was young—gave me hope. As I emerged from my shyness, I was eventually able to act on what my stories said was true about me.

People sometimes take immediate steps after learning what their motivated skills are. Or sometimes this new knowledge can work inside them until they are ready to take action—maybe 10 years later. All the while internal changes can be happening, and people can eventually blossom.

If one advances confidently in the direction of his dreams, and endeavors to live the life which he has imagined, he will meet with success unexpected in common hours.

Henry David Thoreau

Motivated Skills—Your Anchor in a Changing World

Your motivated skills are your anchor in a world of uncertainty. The world will change, but your motivated skills remain constant.

Write them down. Save the list. Over the years, refer to them to make sure you are still on target—doing things that you do well and are motivated to do. As you refer to them, they will influence your life. Five years from now, an opportunity may present itself. In reviewing your list, you will have every confidence that this opportunity is right for you. After all, you have been doing these things since you were a child, you know that you enjoy them, and you do them well!

Knowing our patterns gives us a sense of stability and helps us understand what we have done so far. It also gives us the freedom to try new things regardless of risk or of what others may say, because we can be absolutely sure that this is the way we are. Knowing your patterns gives you both security and flexibility—and you need both to cope in this changing world.

Now think about your own stories. Write down everything that occurs to you.

The Ugly Duckling was so happy and in some way he was glad that he had experienced so much hardship and misery; for now he could fully appreciate his tremendous luck and the great beauty that greeted him....And he rustled his feathers, held his long neck high, and with deep emotion he said: "I never dreamt of so much happiness, when I was the Ugly Duckling!"

Hans Christian Andersen, *The Ugly Duckling*

The Seven Stories Exercise® Worksheet

This exercise is an opportunity to examine the most satisfying experiences of your life and to discover those skills you will want to use as you go forward. You will be looking at the times when you feel you did something particularly well that you also enjoyed doing. Compete this sentence: "There was a time when I…" List enjoyable accomplishments from all parts of your life: from your youth, your school years, your early career up to the present. Don't forget volunteer work, your hobbies and your personal life. Other people may have gotten credit or under-appreciated what you did. Or the result may not have been a roaring success. None of that matters. What matters is that you enjoyed doing it and did it well.

List anything that occurs to you, however insignificant. When I did my own Seven Stories Exercise, I remembered the time when I was 10 years old and led a group of kids in the neighborhood, enjoyed it, and did it well.

When you have 25, select the seven that are most important to you by however you define important. Then rank them: List the most important first, and so on. Starting with your first story, write a paragraph about each accomplishment. Then find out what your accomplishments have in common. If you are having trouble doing the exercises, ask a friend to help you talk them through. Friends tend to be more objective and will probably point out strengths you never realized.

Section I

Briefly outline below *all* the work/personal/life experiences that meet the above definition. Come up with at least 20. We ask for 20 stories so you won't be too selective. Just write down anything that occurs to you, no matter how insignificant it may seem. Complete this sentence, "There was a time when I ..." You may start with, for example, "Threw a fiftieth birthday party for my father," "Wrote a press release that resulted in extensive media coverage," and "Came in third in the Nassau bike race."

Don't just write that you enjoy "cooking." That's an activity, not an accomplishment. An accomplishment occurs at a specific time. You may wind up with *many* cooking accomplishments, for example. But if you simply write "cooking," "writing" or "managing," you will have a hard time thinking of 20 enjoyable accomplishments.

Complete this sentence, "There was a time when I ..."

1. _____
2. _____
3. _____
4. _____
5. _____
6. _____
7. _____
8. _____
9. _____
10. _____
11. _____
12. _____
13. _____

14. _____

15. _____

16. _____

17. _____

18. _____

19. _____

20. _____

21. _____

22. _____

23. _____

24. _____

25. _____

Section II

Choose the seven experiences from the above that you enjoyed the most and felt the most sense of accomplishment about. (Be sure to include non-job-related experiences also.) Then *rank them.* Then, for each accomplishment, describe what *you* did. Be specific, listing each step in detail. Use a separate sheet of paper for each.

Here's how you might begin:

Experience #1: Planned product launch that resulted in 450 letters of intent from 1,500 participants.

a. Worked with president and product managers to discuss product potential and details.

b. Developed promotional plan.

c. Conducted five-week direct-mail campaign prior to conference to create aura of excitement about product.

d. Trained all product demonstrators to make sure they each presented product in same way.

e. Had great product booth built; rented best suite to entertain prospects; conducted campaign at conference by having teasers put under everyone's door every day of conference. Most people wanted to come to our booth.

—and so on—

Analyzing Your Seven Stories

*N*ow it is time to analyze your stories. You are trying to look for the patterns that run through them so that you will know the things you do well that also give you satisfaction. Some of the questions below sound similar. That's okay. They are a catalyst to make you think more deeply about the experience. The questions don't have any hidden psychological significance.

For now, simply go through each story without trying to force it to come out any particular way. Just think hard about yourself. And be as honest as you can. When you have completed this analysis, the words in the next exercise may help you think of additional things. *Do this page first.*

Story #1.

What was the *accomplishment?* _____

What about it did you *enjoy most?*_____

What did you *do best?*_____

What *motivated you to do this?*_____

What about it *made you proud?*_____
What *prompted you to do this?* _____
What *enjoyable skills did you demonstrate?* _____

Story #2.

The accomplishment?_____

Enjoyed most? _____

Did best? _____

A motivator? _____

Made you proud? _____

Prompted you to do this?_____

Enjoyable skills demonstrated? _____

Story #3.

The accomplishment?_____

Enjoyed most? _____

Did best? _____

A motivator? _____

Made you proud? _____

Prompted you to do this?_____

Enjoyable skills demonstrated? _____

Story #4.

The accomplishment? _____

Enjoyed most? _____

Did best? _____

A motivator? _____

Made you proud? _____

Prompted you to do this? _____

Enjoyable skills demonstrated? _____

Story #5.

The accomplishment? _____

Enjoyed most? _____

Did best? _____

A motivator? _____

Made you proud? _____

Prompted you to do this? _____

Enjoyable skills demonstrated? _____

Story #6.

The accomplishment? _____

Enjoyed most? _____

Did best? _____

A motivator? _____

Made you proud? _____

Prompted you to do this? _____

Enjoyable skills demonstrated? _____

Story #7.

The accomplishment? _____

Enjoyed most? _____

Did best? _____

A motivator? _____

Made you proud? _____

Prompted you to do this? _____

Enjoyable skills demonstrated? _____

We are here to be excited from youth to old age, to have an insatiable curiosity about the world. ...We are also here to help others by practicing a friendly attitude. And every person is born for a purpose. Everyone has a God-given potential, in essence, built into them. And if we are to live life to its fullest, we must realize that potential.

Norman Vincent Peale

Let me listen to me and not to them.

Gertrude Stein

What seems different in yourself; that's the rare thing you possess. The one thing that gives each of us his worth, and that's just what we try to suppress. And we claim to love life.

André Gide

Stick with the optimists, Niftie. It's going to be tough enough even if they're right.

James Reston

Optimism Emerges As Best Predictor To Success In Life

"Hope has proven a powerful predictor of outcome in every study we've done so far," said Dr. Charles R. Snyder, a psychologist at the University of Kansas. "Having hope means believing you have both the will and the way to accomplish your goals, whatever they may be. . . . It's not enough to just have the wish for something. You need the means, too. On the other hand, all the skills to solve a problem won't help if you don't have the willpower to do it."

Daniel Goleman, The New York Times, Dec. 24, 1991

Appendix 2

Your Fifteen-Year Vision® and Your Forty-Year Vision®

In my practice as a psychiatrist, I have found that helping people to develop personal gains has proved to be the most effective way to help them cope with problems.

Ari Kiev, M.D., *A Strategy for Daily Living*

If you could imagine your ideal life five years from now, what would it be like? How would it be different from the way it is now? If you made new friends during the next five years, what would they be like? Where would you be living? What would your hobbies and interests be? How about 10 years from now? Twenty? Thirty? Forty? Think about it!

Some people feel locked in by their present circumstances. Many say it is too late for them. But a lot can happen in 5, 10, 20, 30, or 40 years. Reverend King had a dream. His dream helped all of us, but his dream helped him too. He was living according to a vision (which he thought was God's plan for him). *It gave him a purpose in life.* Most successful people have a vision.

A lot can happen to you over the next few decades—and most of what happens is up to you. If you see the rest of your life as boring, I'm sure you will be right. Some people pick the "sensible" route or the one that fits in with how others see them, rather than the one that is best for them.

On the other hand, you can come up with a few scenarios of how your life could unfold. In that case, you will have to do a lot of thinking and a lot of research to figure out which path makes most sense for you and will make you happiest.

When a person finds a vision that is right, the most common reaction is fear. It is often safer to *wish* a better life than to actually go after it.

I know what that's like. It took me two years of thinking and research to figure out the right path for myself—one that included my motivated abilities (Seven Stories Exercise) as well as the sketchy vision I had for myself. Then it took *10 more years* to finally take the plunge and commit to that path—running The Five O'Clock Club. I was 40 years old when I finally took a baby step in the right direction, and I was terrified.

You may be lucky and find it easy to write out your vision of your future.

Or you may be more like me: It may take a while and a lot of hard work. You can speed up the process by reviewing your assessment results with a Five O'Clock Club career counselor. He or she will guide you along. Remember, when I was struggling, the country didn't *have* Five O'Clock Club counselors or even these exercises to guide us.

Test your vision and see if that path seems right for you. Plunge in by researching it and meeting with people in the field. If it is what you want, chances are you will find some way to make it happen. If it is not exactly right, you can modify it later—after you have gathered more information and perhaps gotten more experience.

Start with the Present

Write down, in the present tense, the way your life is right now, and the way you see yourself at each of the time frames listed. **This exercise should take no more than one hour.** Allow your unconscious to tell you what you will be doing in the future. Just quickly comment on each of the questions listed on the following page, and then move on to the next. If you kill yourself off too early (say, at age 60), push it 10 more years to see what would have happened if you had lived. Then push it another 10, just for fun.

When you have finished the exercise, ask yourself how you feel about your entire life as you laid it out in your vision. Some people feel depressed when they see on paper how their lives are going, and they cannot think of a way out. But they feel better when a good friend or a Five O'Clock Club counselor helps them think of a better future to work toward. If you don't like your vision, you are allowed to change it—it's your life. Do what you want with it. Pick the kind of life you want.

Start the exercise with the way things are now so you will be realistic about your future. Now, relax and have a good time going through the years. Don't think too hard. Let's see where you wind up. You have plenty of time to get things done.

🖉 🖉 🖉 🖉 🖉

The 15-year mark proves to be the most important for most people. It's far enough away from the present to allow you to dream.

🖉 🖉 🖉 🖉 🖉

There are more things in heaven and earth, Horatio, than are dreamt of in your philosophy.

William Shakespeare, *Hamlet*

Your Fifteen- and Forty-Year-Vision Worksheet

1. The year is_____(current year). You are _____ years old right now.

Year: _____ Your Age_____

_____

· Tell me what your life is like right now.

_____
_____

(Say anything you want about your life as it is now.)

_____
_____

· Who are your friends? What do they do for a living?

_____
_____

· What is your relationship with your family, however you define "family"?

_____
_____

· Are you married? Single? Children? (list ages.)

_____
_____

· Where are you living? What does it look like?

_____
_____

· What are your hobbies and interests?

_____

· What do you do for exercise?

_____

· How is your health?

_____

· How do you take care of your spiritual needs?

_____
_____

· What kind of work are you doing?

_____

· What else would you like to note about your life right now?

_____

Don't worry if you don't like everything about your life right now. Most people do this exercise because they want to improve themselves. They want to change something? What do you want to change?

Please continue . . .

2. The year is_____(current year + 5).

You are _____years old right now.
(Add 5 to present age.)

Things are going well for you.

• What is your life like now at this age?

(Say anything you want about your life as it is now.)

• Who are your friends? What do they do for a living?

• What is your relationship with your "family"?

• Are you married? Single? Children? (List their ages now.)

• Where are you living? What does it look like?

• What are your hobbies and interests?

• What do you do for exercise?

• How is your health?

• How do you take care of your spiritual needs?

• What kind of work are you doing?

• What else would you like to note about your life right now?

Year: _____ Your Age_____

_____
_____
_____
_____
_____
_____
_____
_____
_____
_____
_____
_____
_____
_____
_____
_____
_____
_____
_____
_____
_____
_____
_____
_____
_____

3. The year is_____(current year +15).   Year: _____ Your Age_____

You are _____years old right now.
(Add 15 to present age.)
Things are going well for you.

• What is your life like now at this age?

(Say anything you want about your life
  as it is now.)

• Who are your friends? What do they
  do for a living?

• What is your relationship with your
  "family"?

• Are you married? Single? Children?
  (List their ages now.)

• Where are you living? What does it
  look like?

• What are your hobbies and interests?

• What do you do for exercise?

• How is your health?

• How do you take care of your
  spiritual needs?

• What kind of work are you doing?

• What else would you like to note
  about your life right now?

The 15-year mark is an especially important one. This age is far enough away from
the present that people often loosen up a bit. It's so far away that it's not threatening. Imagine your ideal life. What is it like? Why were you put here on this earth?
What were you meant to do here? What kind of life were you meant to live? Give
it a try and see what you come up with. If you can't think of anything now, try it
again in a week or so. On the other hand, if you got to the 15-year mark, why not
keep going?

4. The year is **xxxx** (current year +25).
You are _____ years old!
(Current age plus 25.)

🍃🍃🍃🍃🍃🍃🍃🍃🍃🍃🍃🍃🍃🍃🍃🍃🍃🍃🍃🍃🍃🍃🍃

5. The year is **xxxx** (current year +35).
You are _____ years old!
(Current age plus 35.)

🍃🍃🍃🍃🍃🍃🍃🍃🍃🍃🍃🍃🍃🍃🍃🍃🍃🍃🍃🍃🍃🍃🍃

6. The year is **xxxx** (current year +45).
You are _____ years old!
(Current age plus 45.)

🍃🍃🍃🍃🍃🍃🍃🍃🍃🍃🍃🍃🍃🍃🍃🍃🍃🍃🍃🍃🍃🍃🍃

7. The year is **xxxx** (current year +55).
You are _____ years old!
(Current age plus 55.)
(Keep going—don't die until you are past 80!)

🍃🍃🍃🍃🍃🍃🍃🍃🍃🍃🍃🍃🍃🍃🍃🍃🍃🍃🍃🍃🍃🍃

Year: _____ Your Age _____
Using a blank piece of paper, answer all of the questions for this stage of your life.

Repeat

Repeat

Keep going. How do you feel about your life? You are allowed to change the parts
you don't like. _____ _____
_____

You have plenty of time to get done everything you want to do. Imagine wonderful things for yourself. You have plenty of time. Get rid of any "negative program-
ming." For example, if you imagine yourself having poor health because your
parents suffered from poor health, see what you can do about that. If you imagine yourself dying early because that runs in your family, see what would have
happened had you lived longer. It's your life—your only one. As they say, "This is
the real thing. It's not a dress rehearsal."

Index

About the Author

Dr. Richard Bayer is Chief Operating Officer of The Five O'Clock Club and the official spokesperson for the company. He is a frequent guest on radio and TV, having appeared on the *TODAY Show*, CNN, *Good Day New York*, *Fortune Magazine*, Bloomberg News, and other major media.

For seven years, Richard served as a member of the board of directors for Workforce America, The Five O'Clock Club's not-for-profit career coaching organization located in Harlem serving adults who are not yet in the professional or managerial ranks.

For five years, he served as co-chair of The Five O'Clock's 'Employment Roundtable,' an organization of senior executives from government, business, and think tanks, which met to discuss the important employment issues of our time. Members included representatives from organizations such as Time-Warner, the Conference Board and officials from the U.S. Department of Labor.

He currently represents the Club as a professor at Bayview Prison in Manhattan as part of the Learning Center for Women in Prison so inmates will be better prepared for life after prison, thus helping to reduce the recidivism rate.

He has a background of 22 years of teaching at the University level in the areas of economics and ethics. He is a frequent contributor to *The Five O'Clock News*, author of a book on labor economics (Georgetown University Press, 1999), author of 18 articles and reviews in scholarly journals, and numerous popular essays on topics concerning business ethics.

The current book makes use of the popular essays on topics concerning business ethics.

Richard currently lives in Manhattan with his wife.

About the Five O'Clock Club
and the "Fruytagie" Canvas

ive O'Clock Club members are special. We attract upbeat, ambitious, dynamic, intelligent people— and that makes it fun for all of us. Most of our members are professionals, managers, executives, consultants, and free-lancers. We also include recent college graduates and those aiming to get into the professional ranks, as well as people in their 40s, 50s, and even 60s. Most members' salaries range from $30,000 to $400,000 and much more (one-third of our members earn in excess of $100,000 a year). For those who cannot attend a Club, *The Five O'Clock Club Book Series* contains all of our methodologies—and our spirit.

The Philosophy of The Five O'Clock Club

The "Fruytagie" Canvas by Patricia Kelly, depicted at the end of this chapter, symbolizes our philosophy. The original, which is actually 52.5" by 69" inches, hangs in the offices of The Five O'Clock Club in Manhattan. It is reminiscent of popular 16th century Dutch "fruytagie," or fruit tapestries, which depicted abundance and prosperity.

I was attracted to this piece because it seemed to fit the spirit of our people at The Five O'Clock Club. This was confirmed when the artist, who was not aware of what I did for a living, added these words to the canvas: "The gar-den is abundant, prosperous and magical." Later, it took me only 10 minutes to write the blank verse "The Garden of Life," because it came from my heart. The verse reflects our philosophy and describes the kind of people who are members of the Club.

I'm always inspired by Five O'Clock Clubbers. They show others the way through their quiet behavior ...their kindness ...their generosity ...their hard work ...under God's care.

We share what we have with others. We are in this lush, exciting place together—with our brothers and sisters—and reach out for harmony. The garden is abundant. The job market is exciting. And Five O'Clock Clubbers believe that there is enough for everyone.

About the Artist's Method

To create her tapestry-like art, Kelly developed a unique style of stenciling. She hand-draws and hand-cuts each stencil, both in the negative and positive for each image. Her elaborate technique also includes a lengthy multilayering process incorporating Dutch metal leaves and gilding, numerous transparent glazes, paints, and wax pencils.

Kelly also paints the back side of the canvas using multiple washes of reds, violets, and golds. She uses this technique to create a heavy vibration of color, which in turn reflects the color onto the surface of the wall against which the canvas hangs.

The canvas is suspended by a heavy braided silk cord threaded into large brass grommets inserted along the top. Like a tapestry, the hemmed canvas is attached to a gold-gilded dowel with finials. The entire work is hung from a sculpted wall ornament.

Our staff is inspired every day by the tapestry and by the members of The Five O'Clock Club. We all work hard—and have FUN! The garden *is* abundant—with enough for everyone. We wish you lots of success in your career. We—and your fellow members of The Five O'Clock Club—will work with you on it.

—Kate Wendleton, President

The original Five O'Clock Club was formed in Philadelphia in 1883. It was made up of the leaders of the day, who shared their experiences "in a spirit of fellowship and good humor."

 THE GARDEN OF LIFE IS abundant, prosperous and magical. ❦ In this garden, there is enough for everyone. ❦ Share the fruit and the knowledge ❦ Our brothers and we are in this lush, exciting place together. ❦ Let's show others the way. ❦ Kindness. Generosity. ❦ Hard work. ❦ God's care.

FEB 17 2016